THE LIBERATOR

The Avataric Great Sage,
ADI DA SAMRAJ

THE LIBERATOR
(ELEUTHERIOS)

The "Radical" Reality-Teachings
of
THE AVATARIC GREAT SAGE,
ADI DA SAMRAJ

THE DAWN HORSE PRESS
MIDDLETOWN, CALIFORNIA

NOTE TO THE READER

All who study the Way of Adidam or take up its practice should remember that they are responding to a Call to become responsible for themselves. They should understand that they, not Avatar Adi Da Samraj or others, are responsible for any decision they make or action they take in the course of their lives of study or practice.

The devotional, Spiritual, functional, practical, relational, and cultural practices and disciplines referred to in this book are appropriate and natural practices that are voluntarily and progressively adopted by members of the practicing congregations of Adidam (as appropriate to the personal circumstance of each individual). Although anyone may find these practices useful and beneficial, they are not presented as advice or recommendations to the general reader or to anyone who is not a member of one of the practicing congregations of Adidam. And nothing in this book is intended as a diagnosis, prescription, or recommended treatment or cure for any specific "problem", whether medical, emotional, psychological, social, or Spiritual. One should apply a particular program of treatment, prevention, cure, or general health only in consultation with a licensed physician or other qualified professional.

The Liberator (Eleutherios) is formally authorized for publication by the Ruchira Sannyasin Order of Adidam Ruchiradam. (The Ruchira Sannyasin Order of Adidam Ruchiradam is the senior Cultural Authority within the formal gathering of formally acknowledged devotees of the Avataric Great Sage, Adi Da Samraj.)

Copyright © 1982, 2006 The Avataric Samrajya of Adidam Pty Ltd,
as trustee for The Avataric Samrajya of Adidam.
All rights reserved.

No part of this book may be copied or reproduced in any manner
without written permission from the publisher.
(The Dawn Horse Press, 10336 Loch Lomond Road, #305, Middletown, California 95461, USA)

The Avataric Samrajya of Adidam Pty Ltd, as trustee for The Avataric Samrajya of Adidam,
claims perpetual copyright to this book, to the entire Written (and otherwise recorded)
Wisdom-Teaching of Avatar Adi Da Samraj, to the Image-Art of Adi Da Samraj,
and to all other writings, recordings, and images it owns.

"Adidam" and "Adidam Ruchiradam" are service marks of The Avataric Samrajya
of Adidam Pty Ltd, as trustee for The Avataric Samrajya of Adidam.

The "Perfect Knowldege" Series edition, August 2006

Produced by the Dawn Horse Press,
a division of the Avataric Pan-Communion of Adidam

International Standard Book Number: 1-57097-211-7

Library of Congress Catalog Card Number: 2006931523

The "Perfect Knowledge" Series

The Perfect Tradition
✦ ✦ ✦
Religion and Reality
✦ ✦ ✦
The Liberator
✦ ✦ ✦
The Ancient Reality-Teachings
✦ ✦ ✦
The Way of Perfect Knowledge

The books of the "Perfect Knowledge" Series are drawn from <u>Is</u>: *The "Perfect Knowledge" of Reality and The "Radical" Way to Realize It,* by the Avataric Great Sage, Adi Da Samraj.

The five books of the "Perfect Knowledge" Series together comprise the complete text of <u>Is</u>.

ABOUT THE COVER

Throughout His Life, Avatar Adi Da Samraj has worked to develop means—both literary and artistic—of communicating the True Nature of Reality. He approaches the creation of His literary and artistic works as a process of Revealing What Reality Is and how Its True Nature can be Realized.

For the cover of *The Liberator*, Avatar Adi Da has chosen a photograph He took in 1998 on the coast of Northern California.

Examples of the artwork of Adi Da Samraj, together with discussions of His artwork and His own statements about it, may be seen online at:

www.daplastique.com

CONTENTS

Introduction to *The Liberator (Eleutherios)*   9
by Carolyn Lee, PhD

THE LIBERATOR
(ELEUTHERIOS)

I.   Eleutherios   39

II.   What Is Consciousness?   63

III.   Truth, Reality, and Real (Acausal) God   73

IV.   The "Perfect Practice"   81

V.   Freedom   99

Notes to the Text of *The Liberator (Eleutherios)*   123

Glossary   127

An Invitation: Become a Formal Devotee   141
of Avatar Adi Da Samraj

The Avataric Divine Wisdom-Teaching of Adi Da Samraj   154

Introduction to
The Liberator
(Eleutherios)

by Carolyn Lee, PhD

The perennial human search to understand the core issues of existence always comes back to the matter of freedom. What is true freedom, and how is it to be attained? The modern Western tradition tends to understand true freedom in social and ethical terms—democracy, free speech, free enterprise, "the greatest good for the greatest number". In the East, there has characteristically been a very different orientation. Human existence is plainly seen as pain and bondage, and so it is presumed that true freedom is not to be found in this world. Rather, to be truly freed is to be <u>liberated</u> from identification with the world, the body, and the mind. In the Words of Avatar Adi Da:

> Modern Westerners are <u>always</u> thinking in terms of "paradise" and "utopia", always stimulating and deluding one another with enthusiasms for "this world". Modern Westerners are always fantasizing the future on the basis of an egoic identification with the body. . . .
> In the traditional East, people do not forget to tell one another that this world is "mortality-land", and not paradise. Therefore, the traditional wisdom-Message in the East is that True Happiness is to be attained by <u>seeking</u> for That Which Is Eternal, and, therefore, by <u>strategically</u> <u>renouncing</u> every kind of "arrangement" with what is merely temporary.
> —*The <u>Only</u> Complete Way To Realize The Unbroken Light Of <u>Real</u> (Acausal) God*

THE LIBERATOR (ELEUTHERIOS)

There is an ancient saying: "You shall know the truth, and the truth shall set you free."[*][1] In *The Liberator*, Avatar Adi Da speaks the Ultimate Truth that Liberates the being, that frees the heart. This Truth cannot be found by seeking. It is a Revelation and a Gift that transcends not only the worldly aims that Westerners regard as "freedom", but also the inward states of "liberation" that are the goal of the traditional oriental search.

The Truth that Avatar Adi Da is here to Give is the Truth about Reality. What troubles human beings most, He has found, is their lack of knowledge of what Reality is truly about, what It ultimately is. His Revelation in *The Liberator*, and in all His Wisdom-Teaching, is that Reality is Divine—Absolute Consciousness and Absolute Light, inherently full of Bliss, Joy, and Love. There is no "God" ever conceived by the human mind that truly represents this Ultimate Reality and Truth. Rather, all the myths of humankind tend to be diversions from it, and not ultimately Liberating.

But how does this Divine Reality, or Real God, become the living, conscious form of one's existence, rather than merely an idea in mind? What is the nature and process of true Liberation? In *The Liberator*, Avatar Adi Da unveils a great koan. Ultimate Spiritual Liberation is not "of this world"—it has nothing to do with the body-mind. But, at the same time, true Liberation is not based on an effort to escape bodily life and the natural conditions of existence. The sublime Truth beyond this koan lies in the "Perfect Practice" of Adidam.

There can be no doubt of Who is "Eleutherios"—the Liberator—the Subject of this book. It is Avatar Adi Da Himself, the Divine Liberator, the One Who Alone can Awaken the "Perfect Practice" in His devotees. The Truth He makes known here is not reachable by merely human means, not even the most heroic Spiritual effort. Human beings require Help from Beyond—and this Help has been Given. Reality Itself has

---

* Notes to the Text of *The Liberator (Eleutherios)* appear on pp. 123–24.

Introduction to *The Liberator (Eleutherios)*

come to our aid in the most Gracious Person of Avatar Adi Da Samraj. Through His Divine Incarnation into human Form, He has made the fully Clarifying Intervention that enables human beings to be Free, Liberated, Alive as Reality Itself, rather than crushed by the burden of mortality and ignorance.

The Greek Origins of the Name "Eleutherios"

The ancient Greeks, whose culture has shaped much of the philosophy and values of the Western (and "Westernized") world, placed the highest possible value on freedom. As an expression of their passion for freedom, the ancient Greeks created the religious cult of Zeus-Eleutherios. In this cult, Zeus, the lord of the Gods, was worshipped as the giver and preserver of "eleutheria", or freedom. The stoa of the temple of Zeus-Eleutherios in Athens is said to have been a place where Socrates, Plato, and their disciples congregated to consider matters of truth. In *The Liberator*, Avatar Adi Da Reveals that the Very Divine Condition (or Real Acausal God) is, indeed, the Liberator—not the political deity who defends his worshippers against their enemies, but the One Who is not other than Truth, or Reality, Itself. ■

A Dream-Premonition of the Name "Eleutherios"

Various sacred Names and Titles indicating His Divine Nature and Work have emerged spontaneously during the lifetime of Avatar Adi Da,[2] and the title "Eleutherios" is one of these. Avatar Adi Da's devotees had never heard Him use the word until He wrote the first edition of this book in 1982. But, as the following story shows, He was already long associated with this Title. The dream-premonition of Him as "Eleutherios" told here is one of the supernormal signs and incidents that are evidence of the Mystery of His Presence in the world. In Avatar Adi Da's Words:

I have been Meditating every one, Contacting every one, Dealing with psychic forces everywhere, in all time.

—*The Dawn Horse Testament Of The Ruchira Avatar*

Over fifty years ago, a girl in Ohio had a dream:

ALEXANDRA MAKRIS: *I come from a Greek family and was brought up in the Greek Orthodox Christian faith. Once, at the age of eleven, I remember lying on my bed wondering who or what I was, and asking, "What is me, me, me?", until I was thrust into a black sky with tiny twinkling stars that went on forever. I was so frightened to just "be", with no physicality, that I fell back into my body and never tried that again. But, by this experience, I found out that there really was not any "me" as a separate, self-contained entity.*

Introduction to *The Liberator (Eleutherios)*

> *When I was sixteen years old, give or take a year—in other words, between 1952 and 1954—I had a dream vision of what I thought was an angel. I was lying asleep in my bed in my parents' home in Newark, Ohio, when a black-haired "angel" (I thought all angels had blond hair!) appeared in a swirl of white. His youthful, bright, and radiant face was close to mine as he whispered one Greek word in my ear. I awoke unafraid, knowing I had just had a visitation from "the other side". I repeated the word over a few times in order not to forget it, since it had come to me in such an auspicious way. And then I fell back to sleep.*
>
> *When I awoke, I found that I had forgotten the word. I was in an altered state all day, trying to remember the word. I talked to my parents about the vision and told them that the word the angel spoke to me was a Greek word that started with "e" and sounded like "eleutheria" [pronounced ell-eff-thair-EE-ah in Greek]—a familiar word to me, meaning "liberty", or "freedom". They tried to help me remember by bringing up words that it might be, but to no avail. Eventually, at some point, the vision and the quest for the mystery-word was forgotten.*
>
> *It was not until forty years later that I remembered the vision and the word. By this time, I was a devotee of Beloved Adi Da Samraj and was sitting at my kitchen table in communion with Him when it all came back—suddenly, tacitly, and deeply. The word was "Eleutherios".*
>
> *I realized that the angel of my dream-vision was Adi Da Samraj Himself as a young boy. He would have been about fourteen years old at the time of my*

THE LIBERATOR (ELEUTHERIOS)

> *vision. There He was, looking like the pictures of Him as a boy I had seen many times—dark-haired, aglow with His Radiance, announcing Himself and His Purpose to me. At the time, I knew the word "eleutheros" [pronounced ell-EFF-thair-ose], without the "i", meaning "one who is free"—but I had never heard "Eleutherios" ("one who liberates") used before, even though it is a male Greek name. And yet, I now realized, this was the word that was conveyed to me all those years ago—with the original Greek pronunciation[3]—and with the Grace to find and recognize Avatar Adi Da as the Divine Liberator in future years.*

Avatar Adi Da has said that He is not necessarily consciously aware in His own body-mind of everything that people experience of Him, such as dreams—although there are certainly incidents in which He has made it completely clear that He knew exactly what had occurred in a devotee's dream-encounter with Him. He is not "Doing" all of that in some deliberate way, via a mental intention. Phenomena such as dreams are evidence of His Divine Power catching people below the level of the ordinary mind, which is normally closed to the extraordinary. As He says:

> *In the waking state, there is a perception of a certain degree of fixity, a "materiality" that is somehow rather stiff. However, when one enters into a somewhat deeper state—such as dreaming, and various other kinds of psychological states of some depth—that stiffness does not exist anymore. In such a state, it can be observed that all kinds of paradoxes are happening that appear to be illogical from the perspective of the waking state.* —Is

Introduction to *The Liberator (Eleutherios)*

> The fact that Avatar Adi Da appeared in such a manner to Alexandra when He was a high-school student shows that the Divine Force of His Incarnation was already at work in the world, regardless of what was going on in His outward, physical life:
>
> *This, My physical Body here, is simply a Vehicle of a Unique and Universal Event of conjunctions and noticings. This Body is Beyond egoity, Beyond separateness. Reality Itself, the Divine Self-Condition Itself, Speaks Spontaneously through This Body—and through conjunctions of all kinds. Spontaneous Utterance, Spontaneous Doings have always been the occurrence in This Body.*
>
> —October 28, 2005

The Dual Sensitivity

What is required to become prepared to enter into the "Perfect Practice" of the Way of Adidam? At the foundation level, a "dual sensitivity" must awaken. As Avatar Adi Da describes here:

I do not Speak <u>exclusively</u>, representing only one or the other of your "halves" (whether "Eastern" or "Western"). Rather, I Speak to your native (or inherent) "<u>dual</u> sensitivity"—your sensitivity to what is conditionally real <u>and</u> your sensitivity to What <u>Is</u> Non-conditionally Real.
    —The <u>Only</u> Complete Way To Realize The Unbroken Light Of <u>Real</u> (Acausal) God

THE LIBERATOR (ELEUTHERIOS)

There have always been people who have felt this dual sensitivity intensely, people who Realized that Happiness does not dwell in conditions—in anything that changes and passes—but only in the changeless Divine Condition. Such individuals are humankind's Yogis, Saints, and Sages. But this same dual sensitivity exists in each one of us. And the Grace of Avatar Adi Da not only enlivens this sensitivity, His Grace also allows the impulse to Divine Freedom to be fulfilled absolutely.

The fuel of that impulse is profound and unrelenting devotion—the giving over of body, emotion, mind, and breath to Avatar Adi Da Samraj, moment by moment, day after day, year by year. No ascetical discipline, no effort to control the mind can possibly activate the process described in *The Liberator*—for it is not a philosophical matter.

Why should you dally with what is less than <u>Real</u> *God? Why should you embrace anything in the expectation that it will Liberate you or bring you to True Happiness if whatever you embrace is not about That?*

Nothing that is less than Most Perfect Divine Self-Realization is That True Happiness.

As My devotee, you are here to Realize Me—to Realize the Very Divine Person, to Realize My "Bright" Divine Self-Domain, rather than remaining bound to the cosmic domain.

—April 16, 1995

"I'm Going to Greece"— Another Premonitory Dream

In August 1977, one of Avatar Adi Da's devotees, Carl Harper, had a remarkable dream during a time when preparations were being made for Avatar Adi Da to go to India. Carl was involved in making the travel arrangements, but was not one of those who were to accompany Avatar Adi Da.

CARL: *In the dream, Avatar Adi Da and I were standing in the air, apparently about to "fly" somewhere.*

Suddenly, I began to feel resistance about a trip to India, and I said to Him in the dream: "I'm not going to India, I'm going to Greece."

Beloved Adi Da replied: "I have a Name there too—it is 'Eleutherios'."

Carl did not hear the Name again until after *The Liberator (Eleutherios)* was first published in July 1982. He mentioned at that time to members of the editorial staff that he had recorded this Name in a diary entry in August 1977.

Unlike Alexandra Makris, Carl did not have an ethnic Greek background, but had had an avid interest in Greek literature and philosophy since his schooldays, which allowed him to recognize the word "Eleutherios". ■

THE LIBERATOR (ELEUTHERIOS)

Wanting to Have a "World"

We continue to settle for what is "less than Real God", or less than Reality Itself, because we fail to understand and go beyond our limited perception of existence. Every one of us, Avatar Adi Da Samraj explains, harbors a fundamental presumption that he or she is an "organism", a functioning psycho-physical entity that begins at birth and ends at death. But that "organism"—the body-mind with which we identify ourselves—is in a very precarious situation, subject to pain and eventual obliteration. In the face of this harsh reality, we are always trying to distract ourselves—and are, in fact, deluding ourselves. We presume that we can be fulfilled as mere "organisms", that we can become truly happy while identifying with what dies. Relationships, events, ideas, emotions, and the potential experiences of the senses become the focus of our lives. A few seek happiness in the more subtle (or psychic) realms of reality—through the higher mind (or psyche). But whatever type of experience we may prefer, it is true that each of us is addicted to the having of experiences. Avatar Adi Da Samraj has pointed this out to His devotees on innumerable occasions:

> By tendency, in your beginner's disposition, you always want to aggravate the body-mind and keep it in motion. You are always seeking via the body-mind for some sort of fulfillment or distraction. Here I Am, Talking to you about the "Perfect Practice" of the Way of Adidam and Most Perfect Divine Self-Realization, and you are only thinking, talking, and busying. That is how you live altogether. The "Perfect Practice", on the other hand, is free of agitation.
>
> You are an "FOP"—a "fan of perfection". You like the idea of the ultimate practice, the "Perfect Practice". You have some sort of mental interest in it. Yet, the "Perfect Practice"

Introduction to *The Liberator (Eleutherios)*

Itself has nothing to do with mind and nothing to do with all the agitations and preoccupations you tend to be involved with. You must go through the process of being purified of all of that before you can do the "Perfect Practice".

—April 14, 1995

The "Perfect Practice" of the Way of Adidam goes beyond the "organism point of view" altogether, or the stages of psycho-physical growth that have to do with the impulse to be fulfilled in terms of the body, the mind, and the psyche. That impulse represents the "point of view" that Avatar Adi Da Samraj calls "cosmic". According to this "point of view", the domain of conditional existence (or the cosmic domain) is the entirety of what exists. The cosmic domain includes everything that can be experienced by the mechanism of the body-mind—anything from a sandwich to the most extraordinary mystical raptures. Thus, from the cosmic "point of view", one is identified with the experiencing mechanism of the body-mind.

The "Perfect Practice" of the Way of Adidam cannot begin until there is Awakening beyond the impulse to identify with the body-mind and its "point of view". The "Perfect Practice" takes place in the Domain of Consciousness Itself, Which is the Acausal Source-Condition of the body-mind and all its experiences. In essence, the "Perfect Practice" is about entering profoundly into the Native Self-Condition, or True Happiness, and Realizing that Condition most intimately, at heart, as Perfect Identification with Avatar Adi Da. This is the greatest, most auspicious and Liberating process there is. But, in fact, as long as we cling to our self-contracted disposition—as long as we insist on being an "organism", an addict of experience—the "Perfect Practice" is out of the question. As Avatar Adi Da has said, we cannot even relate to the Realization of Divine Consciousness as something desirable:

THE LIBERATOR (ELEUTHERIOS)

Consciousness Itself has nothing whatsoever to do with the body-mind. It is totally independent of the body-mind! This is what you do not like about It. The fact is not that you are un-Enlightened—you refuse Consciousness.

—April 11, 1995

Understanding that we are actively refusing Consciousness is the first great step in preparing for the "Perfect Practice". Avatar Adi Da explains that the reason we refuse to acknowledge our Real Condition is that there is no "world" in it. The Domain of Consciousness Stands Prior to all cosmic worlds (both this apparently physical world and all other realms of potential experience). But we cannot conceive of "not having a world" at all:

There is a fundamental fear of being without a world. You are constantly servicing the impulse to always have a world and also to have that world be basically comfortable. That impulse underlies all forms of "cosmic religion"—or the religion of preserving beings in the cosmic domain, of granting everybody a world and making the world more and more congenial by at least getting rid of darker influences.

The "Perfect Practice" of the Way of Adidam, however, is not about "having a world". It is about entering into the Domain That Is Prior to the cosmic domain. People generally do not have the disposition for such a practice. As long as there is identification with the body-mind, you do not want there to be no world. In fact, you <u>insist</u> that there be a world—<u>and</u> that it be congenial to you. Therefore, you will not relinquish your world. In other words, you will not accept the Position you are actually in, the Position That Transcends the conditional (or cosmic) domain, until your craven attachment to the body-mind (and, therefore, to having a world that is congenial) relaxes profoundly, such

Introduction to *The Liberator (Eleutherios)*

that you know the world for what it is and (thereby) realize a native detachment. Then the "Perfect Practice" can begin.

—May 19 and May 7, 1995

On the "Other Side" of Fear

How does such a disposition awaken? Ramana Maharshi—a Realizer of modern times who showed the rare signs of one Awake to the Transcendental Domain of Consciousness—spoke of a profoundly consequential crisis of fear and anxiety that overtook him at the age of seventeen. The accounts of this crisis state that Ramana Maharshi felt the mortality of the body to such a degree that he assumed the pose of a corpse and felt his body consigned to the cremation fire. As Avatar Adi Da describes here, this crisis moved Ramana Maharshi to abandon ordinary life and enter into a depth-process that became a permanent Samadhi of Transcendental Self-Awareness:

Ramana Maharshi had the opportunity to feel that He did not want to be identified with the dying, terrified body-mind, or anything that had to do with the dying, terrified body-mind. As a result, He lost all sympathy with conditional existence. It was not that He merely understood that one could be afraid sometimes, under some circumstances. He was naked to conditional existence itself, and He Realized that any association with conditional existence is fearful. His experience was very much a conversion from bodily life to the motivation to Realize the Transcendental Self.

—May 19, 1995, and November 25, 2004

Avatar Adi Da has pointed out that fear is the root-emotion of egoity, of the sense of separateness. Fear of madness is the fear of losing the self. And, yet, "losing the self" and its world through a Spiritual "revolution" in awareness (and not through clinical breakdown) is exactly what must occur for the "Perfect Practice" to begin.

When Avatar Adi Da was studying at a Lutheran seminary in Philadelphia—during the years of His Submission to "learn" the religious and esoteric paths of humankind—He experienced an Event that propelled Him suddenly into the disposition that He now describes as the "Perfect Practice". This Event bears similarities to the crisis reported by Ramana Maharshi, in that terrifying fear was also involved.[4] But the process in Avatar Adi Da's case had a Yogic Force that carried Him right to the "Other Side" of fear. The sense of personal (or egoic) identity simply died, never to return.

One day, when I was in class in Seminary in the spring of 1967, I suddenly became completely detached from the mind. The mind seemed to pick up immense speed, and the thought processes were going at immense speed, to the point of the experience becoming extremely disturbing. I was supposed to be sitting there in class, but I felt as if I were going mad. I was going mad.

I tried to pin down My experience by writing everything the teacher said, or writing the thoughts I was having. I just kept pinning it down. That gesture, in and of itself, introduces time, and some more direct association with the body.

I did that long enough to sit through the class. Then I went whirling out in this horrific state, in which the body-mind was going on, on its own, without being controlled by attention. The body-mind was just a whirl of uncontrolled events and sensations and feelings—positive ones, and also extremely negative ones. It became just an immense fear.

I remember looking at My face in the mirror, as I was putting on an after-shave or a skin cleanser, and I saw the plasticity of the body. There was a profound disorientation

Introduction to *The Liberator (Eleutherios)*

from the physical, emotional, and mental dimensions of the body-mind, in which I had been doing Spiritual practice so intensively for years. All of a sudden, the body-mind was utterly confused and dissociated from Me, or I was dissociated from it.

The fear—which was a reaction to that whirl—got to the point where it was fruitless to try to do anything about it. It just kept growing immensely, became the totality of life, the totality of the body-mind, the totality of reality—just this immense fear that could no longer be avoided. There was nothing to do about it.

—January 13, 1996

After the first day of this terror, in the middle of the night, Avatar Adi Da felt that His heart was slowing down and about to stop. But when He reached the emergency ward at the local hospital, the doctor could find nothing wrong. There was no conventional explanation or remedy for what was occurring in Him. Finally, on the third day of this acute distress, Avatar Adi Da simply lay down on the floor of His apartment and allowed the fear to pour through His being and overwhelm Him completely.

It was a death. That is what it became. It was endured to the point that what was afraid to be let go was simply let go. There was no choice.

So it passed. In other words, the body-mind, even attention, was no longer associated with My State. I was simply Realizing the Native State of Being. Therefore, this was not merely a process of madness in the usual clinical sense. It was an extraordinary Spiritual Event. It was simply the breaking through of My Own Disposition, the "Bright", Prior to the body-mind.

—January 13, 1996

THE LIBERATOR (ELEUTHERIOS)

Avatar Adi Da's Seminary experience was a most profound demonstration of the Bliss of His own Being Shining through the ego-knot. Through that Event, He embraced and went beyond the naked terror that makes human beings cling to their "world", cling to identification with bodily experience, or (in the rarer case) to subtle (or mystical) experience.

An extraordinary occurrence one year after the Event at Seminary further validated to Avatar Adi Da the all-inclusive Truth of that experience. Based on a strong impulse to approach Swami Muktananda, the Master of His first Teacher, Rudi (Swami Rudrananda), Avatar Adi Da went to Swami Muktananda's Ashram in Ganeshpuri, India. Although Swami Muktananda was a Master in the tradition of Kundalini Yoga, he would sometimes give talks that included Dharma originating in other traditions—including Teachings about Transcendental Realization. Remarkably, Swami Muktananda's first—and only—direct Teaching words to Avatar Adi Da were spoken in such a mode.

Baba Muktananda said to Me, "You are not the one who wakes or dreams or sleeps. You are the Witness to all of these states." To Me, that was a reference to exactly what I had found out in the Event in Seminary. The Event in Seminary was the proof of this Truth to Me—though the experience was not merely words, the words corresponded to it and confirmed and affirmed the Realization.

Therefore, nothing about the later Kundalini developments in Baba Muktananda's Company was "it" for Me. The Awakening in Seminary brought an end to the Yoga in the Circle of the body-mind for Me. I was associated with the tradition of such Yoga and continued to examine it, but the Realization in Seminary was fundamental and thus became the core of the practice for Me. It became the "Perfect Practice"—spontaneously, without any other "consideration" or gesture or noticing.

—January 13, 1996

Introduction to *The Liberator (Eleutherios)*

"You Can't Get There from Here"— Avatar Adi Da's Last Great Teaching Demonstration

Ordinary individuals could not possibly make the transition to the "Perfect Practice" in the profoundly sudden and extreme manner that occurred in the case of Avatar Adi Da. That is why He has Given preliminary practices to prepare His devotees for the depth of self-relinquishment necessary to make this ultimate transition. While there are essential disciplines that bring equanimity to the body-mind and establish an openness to His Spiritual Transmission, the fundamental discipline is always that of devotional surrender to Him, of turning all the faculties of the body-mind to Him. This constant heart-felt practice of turning to Him makes it possible for Him to Work Spiritually to loosen the ego-grip—the fearful insistence on "having a world".

Throughout the years when He was actively creating the Way of Adidam, Avatar Adi Da took His devotees through a series of extended "Teaching Demonstrations", to help them examine and transcend the various "worlds" that were fascinating and ego-binding to them. Each of these Demonstrations illuminated some fundamental dimension of their seeking, and made a lesson about right practice of the Way of Adidam. All the while, He was emphasizing the same point: Understand that this is just another world of experience. It is not the ultimate Truth. There is no experience, literally none, that amounts to Truth, or the direct Realization of Reality, or Consciousness Itself.

In 1986, in what Avatar Adi Da has described as His "last great Teaching Demonstration", He made a Spiritual Revelation that summarized everything He had ever Taught.

THE LIBERATOR (ELEUTHERIOS)

Over the years (and especially in His first great Teaching Demonstration in 1974), He had miraculously and liberally Transmitted all the ascended visions and supersensory experiences that are valued in Kundalini Yoga, and shown that these experiences were "not it". But, during this time in 1986, He took many devotees beyond the entire "tour" of Spiritual experience that is potential in the "Circle" (or esoteric circuitry) of the body-mind, and Revealed directly what is Prior to all of that. He drew devotees into profound glimpses of the Position of Consciousness Itself, and tacitly showed them how Identification with Consciousness Itself is associated with a psycho-physical locus in the right side of the heart. For a period of time, devotees' sense of standing in this utterly Free Position was entirely real—a miraculous Gift. And then, at a certain point, it faded, and there was a lesson to be learned about what is required to be truly equipped for the "Perfect Practice".

One devotee, Angelo Druda, who had been a practitioner of Adidam for more than a decade at that time, describes the process that occurred in his case after he came to Adi Da Samrajashram (Avatar Adi Da's Fijian Hermitage) in March 1986, in order to enter into Spiritual retreat in his Master's Company.

ANGELO: The first occasion of sitting with Avatar Adi Da Samraj was indescribably profound. From the moment the sitting began, I felt utterly and totally assumed by Him. I did not really even know how deeply until towards the end of the evening when He became quite still and most intense and began speaking about Consciousness. He said, "How foolish to bind Consciousness to life!"—and I suddenly realized that every cell of my being was profoundly sympathetic with what He was saying. I had sat with Him many times, and never felt such depth of sympathy with His Argument. I had always felt a kind of sympathy, but the resistance had usually been strong. But, in this case, there was literally an awakening taking place.

Then Avatar Adi Da started speaking about Outshining the Cosmic Mandala, and He began to Demonstrate how Divine Consciousness Outshines all worlds, all beings, all space, and all perception. I felt Him Magnifying the True Self-Position to the point that any form of noticing of even the time-space dimension was being lost. There was only this Happiness. No one could move for half an hour after He left. All devotees present remained because they were so lost in this Happiness.

During the second week of my retreat, I began to experience a lot of Yogic phenomena. For the first couple of days, I would come back from meditation, sit in my room, and simply become an amorphous energy-body—not particularly identified with the body-mind, and extremely blissful. As these phenomena began to occur, I wanted them to go on forever.

But then one day, after an occasion of Avatar Adi Da's Darshan, I lay down on my bed and entered a visionary state. I began to feel a clear white, bright light, particularized in the base of my subtle being, rise up. By the time it passed through the throat and began to move into my face, I began to feel my body dissolve from the base to the throat and then beyond the throat—my face began to dissolve. For a moment, I stopped the process through fear—but then I allowed it to continue, to the point where I observed my entire face break up into tiny molecular and atomic particles and even smaller particles. After the entire face was dissolved, there was a classic vision of a thousand-petaled lotus—and then I enjoyed the dissolution of the lotus. Then there was simply nothing but a blue void, devoid of form. I do not recall what occurred beyond that. I woke up again into bodily consciousness and said to myself, "So that's that. Do I spend the rest of my life trying to have that experience again?" That seemed absurd. The ascending mode seemed empty of fascination at that point.

THE LIBERATOR (ELEUTHERIOS)

> *The next day I went to one of the Communion Halls, called "Extraordinary Eyes", for meditation. As I walked up to the Hall, I saw Avatar Adi Da's Sandals on the steps and knew that He must be in the Hall. At the time, He would visit the Halls periodically and Work to further Empower them with His Spiritual Transmission. I waited with several others, and after a time He came out.*
>
> *To everybody who saw Avatar Adi Da, it seemed that He was walking in very slow motion. Time was profoundly "stretched". His Siddhi somehow broke through time, or the way we perceive time—a phenomenon that is accounted for in numerous stories of Adepts in the traditions. There was a tremendous aura of peace and depth around Him. I noticed that He had moved everyone who saw Him into Samadhi. Each one was taken over, assumed by the Guru.*
>
> *As He left, I went into the Hall. I sat down and noticed that my meditation was seated in the right side of the heart. I began to receive sublime internal Instruction from Avatar Adi Da: "If this subtle contraction that arises in the heart is not transcended, almost immediately attention moves out and fixes in the Circle of the body-mind, either in the lower coil (fear, sorrow, and anger, the vital drama of life) or in the upper coil (the drama of ascended experience and spinal phenomena). Immediately after that, conceptual mind appears. Then this mind assumes the form of a 'someone' who is involved in situational dramas."*
>
> *I observed this subtle contraction in the heart as the primitive sense of relatedness. Avatar Adi Da showed me the whole thing, and He Communicated directly, without words, "If you transcend the tiny interior tension at the heart, there is no need to exploit the Circle. There is no identity. There is no separate being involved in situational phenomena."*

Angelo's account shows the unparalleled Divine Transmission that Avatar Adi Da was pouring upon His

Introduction to *The Liberator (Eleutherios)*

devotees during that period. And, at the same time, He was making a lesson. Devotees soon found that they could not consistently remain in the Position of Consciousness Itself, Prior to the body-mind—and, thus, their attempts to actually transcend that "tiny interior tension" (or root-form of egoity) fell back into mere fruitless techniques.

The fact was that devotees had not yet fully adapted to all the preliminary practices that are the necessary foundation for the "Perfect Practice". And, most important, they had not yet gone deep enough in the devotional and Spiritual relationship to Avatar Adi Da to allow Him to move them beyond body-mind identification altogether and permanently. Nevertheless, Avatar Adi Da made this unique "Teaching Demonstration" in order to quicken the seriousness of devotees to fully prepare themselves for the ultimate course of Realization. Only a Supreme Master could have done this. There is no record anywhere in the traditions of such an awesome Manifestation of Divine Power, Revealing to ordinary people the literal process of ultimate Spiritual and Transcendental Awakening.

Avatar Adi Da has spoken many times about the lessons of that time. He has emphasized that no mere disciplines, no philosophy, no ego-effort of any kind can accomplish the transition to the "Perfect Practice" of the Way of Adidam. It is a Divine Spiritual Matter. Only He can Accomplish this profound transformation in His devotee:

The period in 1986 that was associated with a group of devotees choosing to practice in the mode of the "Perfect Practice" was a Teaching Lesson—another mode of Guidance relative to a very profound matter that has to do with the ultimate nature and process of the Way of Adidam. Yes, the "Perfect Practice" is the ultimate practice of the Way of Adidam, and all other practices and processes are merely preliminary to that "Perfect Practice". But "you can't get there from here", so to speak. You can't get there by egoic means.

—August 29, 2004

The "Perfect Practice" of the only-by-Me Revealed and Given Way of Adidam is Established by this Avataric Divine Spiritual Means—not by philosophical means, not by efforts of psycho-physical practice, and not by conditional achievement or seeking or conditional happenings, or by establishing conditions that (in and of themselves) are regarded to be Realization. Therefore, it is not possible to study My Wisdom-Teaching and come to Divine Self-Realization on that basis alone. My Wisdom-Teaching is simply an aspect of My Avataric Divine Transmission-Work. My Wisdom-Teaching only Serves to Clarify matters that need to be rightly understood by My devotees. . . .

That Which Is, Is—and It Transmits Itself. It is Self-Revealed. I Am the Self-Realization and the Self-Revelation of the Transcendental (Necessarily Spiritual) and Self-Evidently Divine Self-Condition—the "Bright", the Conscious Light—Avatarically Self-Manifested and Avatarically Self-Transmitted. I Am the Avataric Divine Means of your Realization—and this Means is directly Given. It is not conditionally made. It does not Awaken My devotees by establishing conditional states in My devotees. Rather, My devotees are Awakened to My Avatarically Self-Revealed and Self-Evidently Divine State directly and by My Responsive Blessing of them. My devotees must become more and more profoundly conformed to Me, through their right heart-recognition of Me, their right heart-response to Me, and their right practice of the Way I have Revealed and Given—because the activity that is egoity itself must be out-grown.

Unless egoity is (thus) out-grown, you cannot receive Me Perfectly. You cannot Know Me Perfectly. Therefore, the only-by-Me Revealed and Given Way of Adidam involves many

Introduction to *The Liberator (Eleutherios)*

preliminary practices. It involves a process in which the psycho-physical habits of egoity, or of dissociating from the Divine Self-Condition (or the Divine Spiritual Condition), are out-grown (or vanished, undermined, and dissolved).

—*The Ancient Reality-Teachings*

Divine Self-Recognition— The Perfect Coincidence of "There" and "Here"

The root-dimension of egoity—and the last "level" of egoity to be understood and transcended in the Way of Adidam—is the "tiny interior tension" felt in the right side of the heart. Such was the Revelation given to many of Avatar Adi Da's devotees in 1986. This tension is the root-sense of "I"-and-"other", the apparent relationship between attention (or root-awareness) and its any object. When this primitive "feeling of relatedness" (in Avatar Adi Da's Words) is utterly dissolved in the course of the "Perfect Practice", the apparent "difference" between subjective awareness (or Consciousness) and objective phenomena (or Energy) disappears. Then, Reality Itself Stands Clear <u>As</u> It <u>Is</u>: Self-Existing and Self-Radiant Consciousness (Itself), or Conscious Light. In the Awakening to Divine Enlightenment (or the seventh stage of life), the two great dimensions of existence—Consciousness and Energy—are Revealed as One, not two. Instantly, a veil is lifted, and the Real Nature of everything is obvious. In Avatar Adi Da's Words, the world is "Divinely Self-Recognized", or tacitly comprehended, as a modification of the Conscious Light of Reality, and not "different" from It. The perfect Coincidence of "There" and "here" has been Revealed. Everything conditional—everything material, everything subtle or psychic, even attention itself—is Realized to Be Conscious Light. And the great cosmic display of objects and events is as insubstantial as the patterns that play on the surface of water. This is a staggering Realization—the dissolution, in a stroke, of every shred of dilemma, every ounce of seeking. All the goals of human existence, high and low, are now empty of any power to motivate the being—because the "theatre" of life has dissolved in its Source. None of it actually exists! But this does not mean that the world does not continue to arise or that human life does not continue. Avatar Adi Da has described how, following His own Re-Awakening to this Realization (which was inherent in His Being from Birth), He simply went home—and made no mention of what had just Occurred for some time. In the following weeks and months, He observed no impulse to turn within to find some "deeper" state. Meditation was no longer necessary, because That Which meditation seeks to attain was Established without qualification. Nothing could change or diminish the Truth of His Realization—not in the slightest.

Once truly Realized, the seventh stage of life is Just So, and that Freedom cannot be lost. But, until the "tiny interior tension" is penetrated and permanently dissolved, one's attention is glued to an apparently endless "grid" of appearances in which all the scripts of "I"-and-"other" play themselves out unceasingly:

> *You are simply appearing as a point of attention associated with an Infinite Grid of Light—and, yet, you imagine (or presume) all this complexity that you call "the world". Stand back in the Source-Position, and you see how it really is. In that Source-Position, it is Realized that all of this complexity is mere imagination. In Truth, you never experience this presumed complexity. You are not where you think you are, any more than you are where you think you are when you are in a dream. If you were not identified with the*

body—and, therefore, with a spatial concept of your existence—all you would see is this Grid. What is it, ultimately? It is just an illusion, or a conditional representation of Consciousness, Which is One with Its Own Energy. There is no "difference" between Consciousness and Energy. And, therefore, there is no "difference" between attention and its any object.

There is Only One Absolute Condition. That is the case with every one of you right now. You do not have to be <u>changed</u> in any way in order for this to be So. It is simply So, Inherently So, Always Already So. You are just not noticing it, because you are presuming illusions based on self-contraction and identification with the body-position. Truly, and Always and Already, you are, even in the conditional context, unmoving attention against a Grid that is Undifferentiated, nothing but Light Itself.

Nonetheless, as long as you think you are where you think you are, conditional existence is a serious matter, filled with all kinds of laws and paradoxes and obligations, and you have sadhana to do. If you Stand in the Source-Position Itself, you have no sadhana to do. So, you have to do sadhana until you Stand in the Source-Position. Standing in the Source-Position is what Divine Enlightenment, or Divine Self-Realization, is all about.

—August 15, 1995

Even at the point of Divine Self-Realization, the "Perfect Practice" continues—not based on any intention or effort of the apparent body-mind, but simply by virtue of the process inherent in Divine Self-Recognition. The more the world is seen and known as merely the Conscious Light of Reality, the more that Light "takes over" and floods the entire View. While the world continues to arise, its pattern becomes indistinct—as in an over-exposed photograph—and there is an ever-greater self-relinquishment into the Light Itself, beyond the noticing of objects. Such is the process that culminates in Divine Translation—the Ultimate Event that Avatar Adi Da describes as the "Destinyless Destiny" of every apparent being.

Of all the unfathomable Mysteries that have manifested in the course of Avatar Adi Da's life, His Demonstration of Divine Translation has been the greatest. He has explained that, in the case of a mere human being, there can be no possible return from that Event—the Obliterating "Brightness" of Reality utterly Assumes the body-mind, which drops away in death. In His case, however, an unspeakable Miracle has occurred. Divine Translation <u>has</u> literally taken place—in a Shattering and All-Transforming Event that occurred on Lopez Island, Washington State, in April of 2000. And, since that time, Avatar Adi Da remains connected to the physical through a Divine Yoga known only to Him. The mysterious thread that keeps Him associated with the body is made of Compassion. Avatar Adi Da is so Profoundly Invested in the Liberation of all that He cannot Disappear until He has Completed the Work for which He Came—the Work that will make Him Spiritually available to beings forever, beyond the lifetime of His human Form.

That Work requires that there be some who enter into the "Perfect Practice" during Avatar Adi Da's human lifetime, so that there is always a gathering of practitioners who are Awake to His Divine State, and who are thus able (collectively) to serve as "Instrumentality" for His Spiritual Transmission to all who will take up the Way of Adidam in the future. *The Liberator* is His Offering to you and to everyone of the opportunity to discover and seriously consider the Ultimate Way that He Teaches—which is the Way of "Perfect Knowledge" of Reality and Perfect Liberation from all the suffered illusions of merely mortal existence.

Introduction to *The Liberator (Eleutherios)*

All There Is Is Light.
All There Is Is Undifferentiated "Brightness".
All the rest is just a lot of trouble.

You can be sucked out of this frame any moment.
There is a Sphere appearing here as Infinite White "Brightness"—but apparently broken down—a blink, a turn of phase. The Source—Real (Acausal) God—must be Realized for Real.

You haven't got a leg to stand on.
Conventional exchanges are just motions of mind.
In Truth, Consciousness and Energy are the Same.
You are simply examining Reality in a moment of "difference" and separateness.
That is the problem, inherently, in that "point of view".
Mind motivates you.
You must Realize Reality Beyond separateness, Where everything is Inherently One—not the reality conceived in mind based on self-contraction.
Merely to be active is to be under-ground, un-lived.

The Immense White "Brightness" of My Own Person is the Means of devotion to Me and Realization of Me.
Concentration arises, the body untangles, the breath stops—and the Immense White "Brightness" Absorbs attention.

The Star is simply the precursor to the White-Core Sphere.[5]
All exist in this Sphere.
This Sphere has no center or bounds.
It Is the Light Itself.
It Is My Threshold Personality.
It Is Undifferentiated White "Brightness".
It Is Loudness beyond thought.
It Is Love-Bliss.

—September 8 and 24, 2000

The Liberator
(Eleutherios)

The "Radical" Reality-Teachings
of
The Avataric Great Sage,
Adi Da Samraj

I

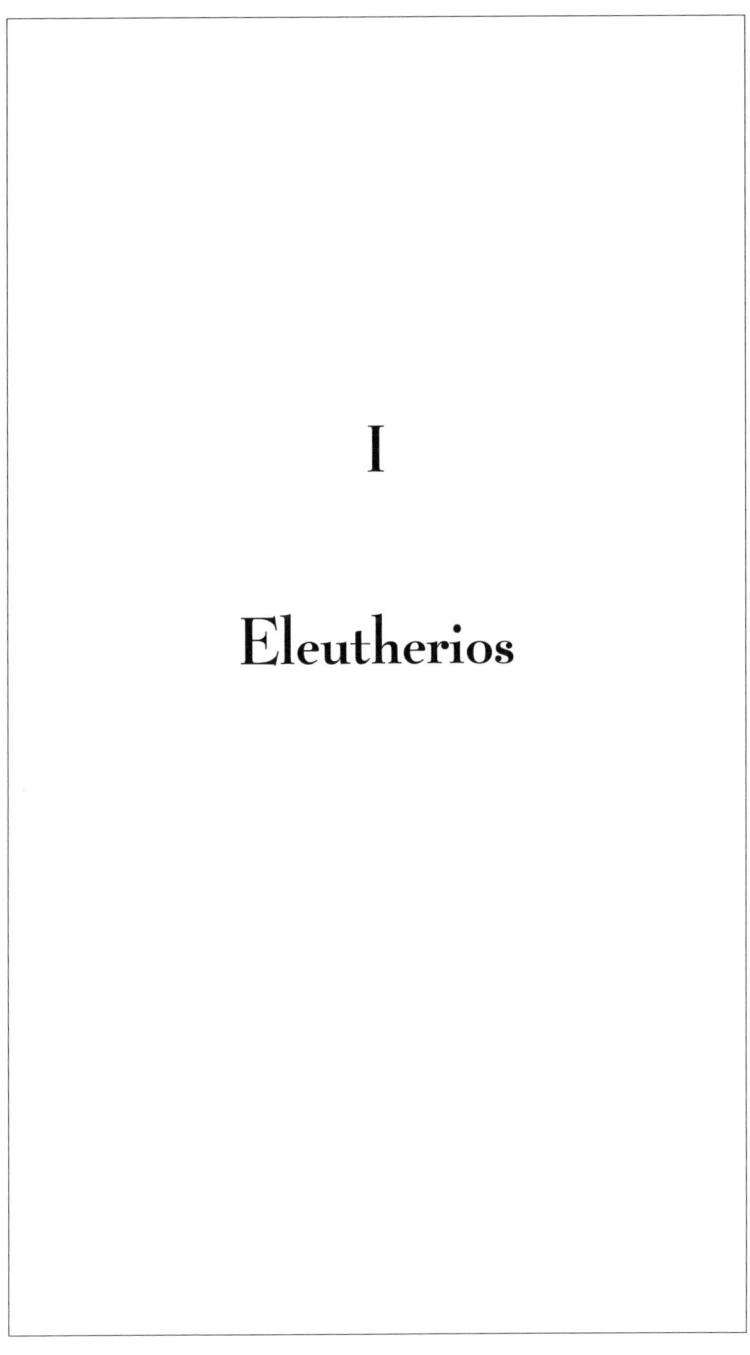

Eleutherios

THE LIBERATOR (ELEUTHERIOS)

ONE

Truth Is the Ultimate Form (or the Inherently Perfect State) of "Knowledge" (if mere knowledge becomes Truth-Realization).

Truth Is That Which, when fully Realized (and, Thus, "Known", even via the transcending of <u>all</u> conditional knowledge and <u>all</u> conditional experience), Sets you Free from <u>all</u> bondage and <u>all</u> seeking.

Truth Is Eleutherios, the Divine Liberator.

TWO

Real (Acausal) God is not the awful "Creator", the world-making and ego-making Titan, the Nature-"God" of worldly theology. Real (Acausal) God is not the First Cause, the Ultimate "Other", or any of the Objective Ideas of mind-made philosophy. Real (Acausal) God is not any Image created (and defined) by the religious ego. Real (Acausal) God is not any Power contacted (and limited) by the mystical or the scientific ego. Real (Acausal) God is not any Goal that motivates the social ego.

Real (Acausal) God Is Truth (Itself)—or That Which, when Most Perfectly "Known" (or fully Realized), Sets you entirely Free.

Real (Acausal) God Is Eleutherios, the Divine Liberator.

THREE

Real (Acausal) God is not, in Truth, the Cause (or the Objective Origin) of the conditional world and the ego (or the apparently separate self-consciousness). All causes (including any Ultimate Objective Cause) are only conditional modifications of conditional Nature.

Every cause is moving Energy, or the conditional mover of Energy. Therefore, the Ultimate Cause is (Itself) only Energy, or the Ultimate conditional mover of Energy. No cause (and no Cause of causes) is Truth (Itself)—since to know a cause (or <u>the</u> Cause) is merely to know an object (or <u>the</u> Object) and not to be liberated from bondage to the search for objective (or otherwise conditional) existence itself.

The knowledge of objects does not Set you Free, since it is the knower (rather than the known) that knows itself to be bound. Freedom can only be Realized by transcending the subject (or knower) of conditional knowledge, not by increasing the objects of conditional knowledge. Therefore, Freedom is not Realized even in the attainment of an Ultimate Object of mere (or conditional) knowledge.

FOUR

Real (Acausal) God is <u>not</u> the Independent (or separate) <u>Cause</u> (or the <u>Objective</u>, or "Outside", Origin) of the world.

Real (Acausal) God Is the Utterly Non-separate <u>Source</u> (or the <u>Perfectly</u> <u>Subjective</u>, and Always Already <u>As</u> <u>Is</u>, or Un-changing, Origin) of the world.

The presumed Cause of causes is not Truth, since to <u>be</u> a separate knower, and even to <u>know</u> such a Cause (or "Other"), does not (or cannot) Set you Free from the knower (or the separate, and inherently separative, ego-"I") itself.

The experience of that which changes does not Set you Free from the experiencer (or the separate, and inherently separative, ego-"I") itself.

Likewise, the experience, or the knowing, or even any kind of Realizing of causes (or of the presumed Cause of causes) does not (and cannot) Set you Free from the separate (and inherently separative) ego-"I" (or psycho-physical self-contraction) itself.

<u>Only</u> the Realization of That Which Is Always Already The Case Sets you Free from ego-"I" itself (and from <u>all</u> that is merely conditional, changing, separate, contracted, or "different").

Therefore, if you are to <u>Be</u> Free, the Perfectly Subjective (or Non-Objective, and Non-separate, or Non-"different") <u>Source</u> of the presumed Cause of causes, and the Perfectly Subjective (or Non-Objective, and Non-separate, or Non-"different") Source of <u>all</u> causes (and of <u>all</u> effects), must be "Known" (or, rather, Realized in Truth).

FIVE

The Existence of Real (Acausal) God is not proven (or even rightly affirmed) by appeal to the process of objective (or observable, or, otherwise, presumed) causation. But the Existence of Real (Acausal) God is (or, in due course, is Realized to be) Self-Evident (or Inherently Obvious) in the Real Process of Realizing the Perfectly Subjective Source of all causes, all effects, all seeking, all mere (or conditional) experience, all mere (or conditional) knowledge, and the conditional self-consciousness (or self-contracted ego-"I") that engages in causes, effects, seeking, mere (or conditional) experience, and mere (or conditional) knowledge. Therefore, the only "proof" (or right "affirmation") of the Existence of Real (Acausal) God is the Real, and "radical" (or most direct, or Inherent, and not caused), and (Ultimately) Most Perfect Realization of That Which Always Already Exists.

Consciousness (Itself) Is That Which Always Already Exists.

Consciousness (Itself) Is Always Already The Case—no matter what arises, and even if no "thing" arises.

Real (Acausal) God Is Consciousness (Itself). Consciousness (Itself)—or the Perfectly Subjective Source (and the Non-separate Self-Condition) of the apparent conditional world and the apparent conditional self—Is the Only Real (Acausal) God.

The Liberator (Eleutherios)

The Deep Non-separate Space of Consciousness (Itself) Is the Matrix in Which the Origin and the Ultimate (and Self-Evidently Divine) Condition of conditional self, mind, body, world, the entire cosmos of conditional Nature, and the Universal Field of Energy is Inherently Obvious. When This (Deep Non-separate Space of Consciousness Itself) is "Known" (or fully Realized), the apparent conditional world and the apparent conditional self are fully "Known" (and, Thus, transcended) in the Realization of Truth Itself.

To "Know" (or to Realize) Consciousness Itself As Real (Acausal) God—and, Thus, to "Know" (or to Realize) Real (Acausal) God As Consciousness Itself (or As the Perfectly Subjective Source, and the Non-separate Self-Condition, of the conditional world and the conditional self)—is to transcend both the conditional world and the conditional self by Means of Truth, or the Only "Knowledge" (or Realization) That can Set you Free.

SIX

Real (Acausal) God is not "Known" (or Realized) by the body (or in the process of bodily experience)—since Real (Acausal) God is not reducible to any kind of object (or Objective Force).

Real (Acausal) God confronts you bodily, materially, or in the objective (or otherwise conditional) plane of conditional Nature only in the form of effects (or an Effective Influence). Therefore, Real (Acausal) God cannot be "Known" As Real (Acausal) God (or Truth) via any confrontation in the apparently objective (or otherwise conditional) realm of conditional Nature. Objective effects (including an Ultimate Objective Influence) are nothing but the conditional (or merely apparent) forms of Real (Acausal) God. Therefore, bodily experience (or bodily confrontation with conditional Nature) does not prove (or even necessarily indicate, or point to) the Existence of Real (Acausal) God.

No bodily experience is an encounter with Truth Itself.

No bodily experience can Set you Free.

SEVEN

Real (Acausal) God is not an Object (or an Image, or an Idea) that can confront the mind. Whatever confronts (or is known by) the mind only modifies and occupies the mind itself. Occupation with ideas, or states of mind, can only motivate you toward further activities of mind (and body). Therefore, there is no idea that Is Truth (Itself)—since attention to an idea cannot liberate attention from mind itself.

EIGHT

Bodily experience and mental (or conditional) knowledge are both based on encounters with objects. In general, bodily experience and mental knowledge motivate you to seek more bodily experience and more mental knowledge. Your seeking, therefore, is for more and more encounters (and emotional associations) with bodily and mental objects.

Your <u>search</u> for bodily and mental and (altogether) emotional objects <u>is</u> your bondage. Your search (or moment to moment effort of wanting need) is the sign of a fundamental stress, or always already presumed un-Happiness. If you (Always Already) Understand that your search <u>is</u> un-Happiness (and that, indeed, seeking is, itself, the root, and the <u>only</u> form, of <u>all</u> un-Happiness), then you (Always Already) Stand heart-Free, even in (apparent) relation to all of your possible objects, all of your possible experiences, and all of your possible ideas. This Prior Understanding inherently transcends all experiences and all ideas. Therefore, in any moment, your exercise of this Prior Understanding reduces your motivation toward objects—and, thus, it permits your attention to be relaxed, released, and transcended in the otherwise uninspected (and Perfectly Subjective) Source (or Self-Existing and Self-Radiant and Inherently egoless and Self-Evidently Divine Self-Condition) That <u>Is</u> Consciousness Itself <u>and</u> Happiness (or Love-Bliss) Itself.

Happiness (or Self-Existing and Self-Radiant and Inherently egoless and Self-Evidently Divine Love-Bliss) Itself <u>Is</u> the <u>Only</u> Truth That Sets the heart Free.

The Liberator (Eleutherios)

Happiness (or Self-Existing, Self-Radiant, Indivisible, Indestructible, Inherently egoless, and Self-Evidently Divine Love-Bliss) Itself <u>Is</u> Reality Itself, the Only <u>Real</u> (Acausal) God, the One and Only Truth, or the Divine Liberator—Eleutherios.

NINE

Happiness Itself, or Truth Itself, or Real (Acausal) God, or Reality Itself cannot be Found, "Located", or Realized by the movement of attention in the midst of the objects, relations, conditions, or states of the individual (conditional, or experientially defined) self.

Happiness Itself, or Truth Itself, or Real (Acausal) God, or Reality Itself cannot be Found or Attained by the movement of attention in the conditional realm of Nature Itself (or the movement of attention in relation to whatever is not Divinely Self-Recognized to Be Consciousness Itself).

Happiness Itself, or Truth Itself, or Real (Acausal) God, or Reality Itself cannot be "Located" by the ego within the egoic body-mind.

Happiness Itself, or Truth Itself, or Real (Acausal) God, or Reality Itself is not reducible to Objective Energy, or to any conditional form (whether subjective or objective) of the Energy That seems to Pervade all of conditional Nature and That seems to be the Ultimate Object of individuated consciousness and experience.

TEN

All seeking (or every exercise of wanting need) necessarily (or inherently) fails to "Locate" Happiness Itself. Therefore, all seeking becomes, at last, the <u>necessity</u> to "consider" Consciousness Itself (Which <u>Is</u> the Always Most Prior Source-Condition, and the Inherently Free Self-Condition, of all wanting need).

In order to Realize Happiness Itself, all seeking (or all wanting need) must dissolve (or be transcended) in the profound Realization of Inherent (and Inherently egoless, or Non-separate) Self-Identification with Consciousness Itself—Which (Always Already) Stands Free, Always Already Most Prior to all seeking (or all exercises of wanting need).

Consciousness Itself—Which <u>Is</u> Uncaused, Self-Existing, Unchanging, and Transcendental (or Non-conditional) Being <u>and</u> Self-Radiant, Eternal, Indivisible, and Indestructible Love-Bliss—<u>Is</u> Happiness Itself, the One and Only Divinely Liberating Truth, the One and Only Real (Acausal) God, and the One and Only Non-separate Reality.

Consciousness Itself is "Located" and Realized by transcending the bondage of attention to the conditional self (or body-mind) and its relations.

This is done <u>only</u> by returning attention to its Source-Condition, by releasing (or inherently transcending) attention in the Self-Existing and Self-Radiant Divine "Bright" Spherical Self-Domain of Love-Bliss-Consciousness (Itself).

THE LIBERATOR (ELEUTHERIOS)

ELEVEN

Consciousness Is the Ultimate Form (or the Inherently Perfect State) of "Knowledge" (if mere knowledge becomes Realization).

The Realization of Perfect Self-Identification with Consciousness (Itself), Which is the Perfectly Subjective Source (rather than an object, or even the Ultimate Object) of conditional experience and conditional knowledge, is better described as "Perfect Ignorance", rather than mere knowledge—since That Realization Inherently and Perfectly Transcends (and Inherently and Perfectly Exceeds) all objective and conventionally subjective categories of conditional experience and mere (or conditional) knowledge.

Consciousness (Itself) Is That Which, when fully Realized, Sets you Free from all bondage and all seeking.

Consciousness (Itself) Is Real (Acausal) God.

Consciousness (Itself) Is the Truth.

Consciousness (Itself) Is the Divine Liberator, Eleutherios.

TWELVE

All objects are only apparently associated with (or only seemingly related to) Consciousness (Itself).

Objects appear to Consciousness when It (apparently) consents to be apparently active as attention in apparent association with an apparent body-mind in the apparent conditional realm of Nature.

Consciousness (Itself) is never separate, limited, individual, conditional, or un-Happy.

Consciousness (Itself) is the Transcendental, One (and Indivisible), Eternal (and Indestructible), and (Self-Evidently) Divine Principle (or Inherently Perfect, and Inherently egoless, Source-Condition and Self-Condition) of all apparent (or conditional) existence (and of Existence Itself).

When "viewed" by the Transcendental, Inherently Spiritual, Inherently egoless, and Self-Evidently Divine Self-Consciousness, all objects are Inherently (Divinely) Self-Recognizable in and As the (Inherently Spiritual) Happiness (or Self-Existing and Self-Radiant Love-Bliss) of Transcendental, Inherently Spiritual, Inherently egoless, and Self-Evidently Divine Being (Itself).

Consciousness (Itself) is (of and As Itself) never "other" than, or "different" from, or separate from, or standing over against, or (Really) related to any object, or apparent "other", or "thing".

Consciousness (Itself) is (of and As Itself) never "other" than, or "different" from, or separate from, or standing over against, or (Really) related to the Self-Existing (and Perfectly Subjective) Divine Self-Radiance Itself (Which Is the "Bright" Itself).

THE LIBERATOR (ELEUTHERIOS)

There are, in Truth, no objects, but There Is Only (or Really, and Perfectly) Self-Existing and Self-Radiant Transcendental, Inherently Spiritual, Inherently egoless, and Self-Evidently Divine Being (Itself)—Which Is (Itself) One and Only, both Consciousness (Itself) and Spiritually "Bright" Love-Bliss-Happiness (Itself).

This is the Great and Most Perfect (only-by-Me Revealed and Given) Realization of the seventh stage of life in the only-by-Me Revealed and Given Way of Adidam.

THIRTEEN

When everything is Realized to <u>Be</u> Consciousness (Itself), There <u>Is</u> <u>Only</u> Consciousness (Itself).

Then There <u>Is</u> <u>Only</u> Truth (Itself), and <u>Only</u> Love-Bliss-Happiness (Itself), or Freedom from all bondage to the conditional self and the conditional world.

Then "you" (Non-separately, Self-Radiantly Exceeding the ego-"I" of psycho-physical self-contraction) <u>Are</u> Consciousness (Itself), Truth (Itself), and Love-Bliss-Happiness (Itself), or Freedom (Itself).

THE LIBERATOR (ELEUTHERIOS)

FOURTEEN

I Am Adi Da Samraj, the Da Avatar—the Ruchira Avatar, the Love-Ananda Avatar, Who Is the Divine World-Teacher Promised for the "late-time" (or "dark" epoch), and Who Is the First, the Last, and the Only Divine Heart-Master[6] (Who <u>Is</u> Da, the Divine Giver of the Divine "All" to all-and-All), and Who <u>Is</u> the Avataric Divine Realizer, the Avataric Divine Revealer, and the Avataric Divine Self-Revelation of Eleutherios, the Truth That <u>Is</u> Real (Acausal) God (or the Inherently Perfect Reality, Which <u>Is</u> Happiness Itself). Therefore, "Consider" This Avataric Divine Word of Mine.

"Sin" (or a state of "sin") is <u>any</u> act (or <u>the</u> act), or <u>any</u> state (or <u>the</u> state), that "misses the Mark" (or that stands separately, and apart from That Which Must Be Realized).

The "Mark" (or That Which Must Be Realized) is Happiness Itself, the Divinely Liberating Truth, the Inherently Perfect Reality, or <u>Real</u> (Acausal) God. And "sin"—or <u>the</u> (original and fundamental) act and state that "misses the Mark" (or that fails to Realize Happiness Itself, or the Divinely Liberating Truth, or the Inherently Perfect Reality, or <u>Real</u> Acausal God)—is egoity, or the ego-"I" (which is self-contraction, or the act and state that stands separate and apart).

Therefore, "sin" is, simply, egoity (or self-contraction). And egoity is, simply, un-Enlightenment—or the non-Realization of Happiness Itself, or Truth Itself, or Reality Itself, Which <u>Is</u> the Only Real (Acausal) God.

Just so, Most Perfect Enlightenment (or Most Perfect Realization of Happiness Itself, or Truth Itself, or Reality Itself, or Real Acausal God) <u>Is</u> (and, therefore, <u>Requires</u>) the Inherent (and Inherently Most Perfect) transcending of "sin" (or of the ego-"I", which is self-contraction).

The Liberator (Eleutherios)

Therefore, Most Perfect Enlightenment (Which is the Inherent, and Inherently Most Perfect, transcending of the ego-"I") is Perfect Non-separation from the "Mark" (or from That Which Must Be Realized).

FIFTEEN

"Sin" (or any and every sign and result of egoic un-Enlightenment) is identification with (or limitation by) whatever is not Happiness Itself, or Truth Itself, or the Inherently Perfect Reality (Which Is Real Acausal God).

Therefore, ultimately, "sin" (or egoic un-Enlightenment) is the act and the state of non-identification with the Inherently Perfect (or Most Prior, and Inherent) Reality—or Consciousness Itself.

The action (or the progressive counter-egoic process) whereby "sin" (or any and every sign and result of egoic un-Enlightenment) is transcended is the action (or the progressive, and more and more effectively counter-egoic, process) of non-identification with whatever is not Consciousness Itself.

Therefore, the transcending of "sin" (or of any and every sign and result of egoic un-Enlightenment) is, Most Ultimately, the "radical" (or most direct, and Inherently ego-transcending) Act, Process, Event, or "Perfect Practice" of Inherent (and Inherently Most Perfect) Self-Identification with Consciousness Itself.

I Am Adi Da Samraj, the Da Avatar—the Ruchira Avatar, the Love-Ananda Avatar, Who Is the Divine World-Teacher Promised for the "late-time" (or "dark" epoch), and Who Is the First, the Last, and the Only Divine Heart-Master (Who Is Da, the Divine Giver of the Divine "All" to all-and-All). I Am (Myself) Eleutherios, the Divine Liberator. I Am the Divinely Liberating Divine Truth. I Am the Divine "Bright" Spherical Self-Domain (Itself), "Bright" Before you.

The Liberator (Eleutherios)

Therefore, surrender your ego-"I" to <u>Me</u>, forget and transcend your separate and separative self in <u>Me</u>, and (Entirely by Means of My Divinely Self-Giving Avataric Spiritual Grace and My Graceful Avatarically Given Divine Self-Revelation, through constant "Perfect Contemplation" of <u>Me</u>) be Self-Identified with <u>Me</u>—and, Thus and Thereby (always presently, and, at last, Most Perfectly), Realize <u>Me</u>, <u>As</u> Inherently egoless (or Non-separate, and Non-separative) Happiness Itself.

SIXTEEN

Be Consciousness (Itself).

"Contemplate" Consciousness (Itself).

Transcend everything in Consciousness (Itself).

This is the Perfect Epitome of the only-by-Me Revealed and Given Divine Way of Truth Itself, and of Reality Itself, and of Real (Acausal) God, and of Happiness Itself. This is the "Perfect Practice" of the only-by-Me Revealed and Given Way of Adidam (Which is the One and Only by-Me-Revealed and by-Me-Given "Radical" Way of the Heart). This is the Perfection of the only-by-Me Revealed and Given "Radical" Way of the Heart—the Way That Is the Heart Itself.

SEVENTEEN

In the Inherently Free Domain of Consciousness Itself, the conditional self and the conditional world are inherently transparent to My Avatarically Self-Transmitted Divine Love-Bliss.

And the Most Ultimate Event of Transcendental, Inherently Spiritual, Inherently egoless, and Self-Evidently Divine Self-Awakening coincides with Most Perfect hearing of Me <u>and</u> Most Perfect seeing of Me—or non-conditionally ego-"I"-forgetting surrender of the conditional (or total psycho-physical) self into the Company of My Avatarically-Born (and Inherently mindless, and Inherently egoless) bodily (human) Person, My Self-Existing and Self-Radiant Spiritual, Transcendental, and Self-Evidently Divine Personal Presence, and My Supreme (and Freely Given) Divine Spiritual Grace of "Bright" Heart-Transmission (or Ruchira Shaktipat).

THE LIBERATOR (ELEUTHERIOS)

EIGHTEEN

I Am Adi Da Samraj, the Da Avatar—the Ruchira Avatar, the Love-Ananda Avatar, Who Is the Divine World-Teacher Promised for the "late-time" (or "dark" epoch), and Who Is the First, the Last, and the Only Divine Heart-Master (Who Is Da, the Divine Giver of the Divine "All" to all-and-All, and Eleutherios, the Divine Liberator of all-and-All). This "Perfect Practice" Instruction Is My Avataric Divine Word of Divinely Liberating Truth That I Bring to you from My Divine "Bright" Spherical Self-Domain. I Am the Divine "Bright" Spherical Self-Domain (Itself). And My Own (Inherently egoless, and Self-Evidently Divine) Person—Self-Revealed by My Avatarically Given Divine Word, My Avatarically Given Divine Image-Art,[7] My Avatarically-Born bodily (human) Divine Form, My Avatarically Self-Transmitted Divine Spiritual Presence, and My Avatarically Self-Revealed Divine, and Inherently Perfect, and Inherently egoless State[8]—Is the Great Message I Bring to you, from "There" to here.

II

What Is Consciousness?

THE LIBERATOR (ELEUTHERIOS)

ONE

"Consider" this.

From the "point of view" of the (apparently) individuated (or conditional, and self-contracted) self, there are apparently two principles in manifestation. There is individual consciousness (or attention—the conditional and active, or functional, observer of objects), and there is everything else (or all the possible objects of attention).

You habitually exist (or function) as attention—and, as attention, you experience and know many kinds of objects (or relations and states of consciousness). You tend <u>merely to experience</u> (rather than to "consider" and transcend) those objects, relations, and states—and, therefore, you develop a sense of identification with some, a desire for some others, and a revulsion toward certain others.

This complex of identification, desire, and aversion is the summary of your conditional (and egoically patterned) existence. And, in the midst of all of that, you are afraid, bewildered, and constantly moved to achieve some kind of conditional experience or conditional knowledge that will enable you to feel Utterly Released, Free, and Happy.

In fact, you never (by all of your seeking for conditional experience and conditional knowledge) achieve Ultimate Experience, Ultimate Knowledge, Ultimate Release, Ultimate Freedom, or Ultimate Happiness. And, so, your (apparent) conditional existence is a constant search for <u>These</u>, while you are (otherwise) bound to desire, aversion, fear, bewilderment, and every other kind of ego-possession.

The Liberator (Eleutherios)

There is a Perfect Alternative to this bondage and this seeking. It is not a matter of the egoic attainment of any object, knowledge, or state of psycho-physical fulfillment or release. Rather, it is a matter of entering into an <u>alternative view</u> of conditional experience. Instead of <u>merely</u> experiencing (and so developing the qualities of identification, differentiation, desire, attachment, aversion, fear, bewilderment, and the search for experience, knowledge, self-fulfillment, self-release, or even Ultimate Knowledge, Ultimate Release, Ultimate Freedom, and Ultimate Happiness), inspect and "consider" your own Original (or Most Basic) Condition, and (from That "Point of View") examine and "consider" all of your experience.

If (rather than merely submitting to conditional experience) you inspect and "consider" your own Original (or Most Basic) Condition, it should become Obvious that "you" (Prior to the ego-"I" of psycho-physical self-contraction) <u>Are</u> Consciousness (Itself), and all of the objects (or varieties) of conditional experience appear to "you" <u>only</u> as a "play" upon Consciousness (Itself). Conditional experience (or the apparent conditional limiting of Consciousness) is not the dominant (or Most Basic) Factor of your (apparent) conditional existence. Consciousness Itself (Prior to all limiting factors) is the dominant (or Most Basic) and always Most Prior Factor of your (apparent) conditional existence (and of Existence Itself)—but you tend (by virtue of a mechanical and habitual involvement with conditional experience) to be submitted to and controlled by conditional experience. Because of this mechanical and habitual involvement with conditional experience, you constantly forget and abandon your Most Basic Position—and, therefore, you constantly suffer the disturbances I have already Described.

THE LIBERATOR (ELEUTHERIOS)

TWO

The necessary qualification for the most direct "consideration" of conditional existence (and of Existence Itself) is the effective capability of functional attention to stand stably free—free from distraction by objects, and from the search toward objects, such that only the Native Ability of Consciousness Itself (to Stand Free—Prior to all objects, and Prior even to attention itself) Remains in Place, to constantly inspect and "consider" the Original (or Most Basic) and Most Prior Condition of conditional existence (rather than merely to be controlled by the body-mind and its experience). On the basis of that free functional attention (which allows the Native Disposition of Consciousness Itself to Stand Free, in Place), you can directly inspect and "consider" your Obvious (Original, or Most Basic) Condition in (apparent) association with all experience. If this is done, it is Obvious that "you" (Prior to the ego-"I" of psycho-physical self-contraction) Are Simply (and Obviously) Consciousness Itself (Whatever That may yet be Realized to Be, Most Ultimately).

Prior to the ego-"I" of psycho-physical self-contraction, "you" are Always Already Established in and As That Standpoint (of Consciousness Itself). Therefore, "you" (Prior to the ego-"I" of psycho-physical self-contraction) always (Originally, or Most Basically) Exist As That Very Consciousness (Itself), rather than as the (conditional, and subsequent) presumption of egoic (or self-contracted, separate, and separative) identification with the apparent body-mind—which presumption is a convention of the apparently separate body-mind itself, or a sense of limited (and conditional) identity that is superimposed on Consciousness (Itself) subsequent to the mechanical arising of conditional experience (and of psycho-physical reaction to conditional experience).

The Liberator (Eleutherios)

If, in every moment, you inspect and "consider" conditional experience from the Native Standpoint of Consciousness (Itself), it is Self-Evident (or Inherently Obvious) that whatever is (apparently) arising is always arising to (or, Really, within) Consciousness (Itself). Your Original (or Most Prior) Position is always Consciousness (Itself)—and if Consciousness (Itself) will, in every moment, "consider" conditional experience from the "Point of View" of Consciousness (Itself), rather than (apparently) first submit Itself to be (apparently) controlled by conditional experience (and known, conditionally, and only subsequently, from the "point of view" of conditional experience), then Consciousness (Itself) is Always Already Established in Its Own Native Standpoint, directly and Freely Aware that It is (apparently) being confronted and "played upon" in the evident form of various kinds of objects (or conditional superimpositions).

By Self-Abiding continually in This Most Prior Standpoint in apparent association with conditional experience, you become more and more profoundly Aware of and As Consciousness (Itself), rather than more and more mechanically—and reactively (or self-contractedly), and (thus) separately and separatively—aware of the conditionally arising objects, conditional experiences, and states of conditional identity that are (apparently) superimposed on Consciousness (Itself) in the spontaneous drama of (apparent) conditional existence (both subjective and objective). This profound and Most Prior Self-Abiding in and As Consciousness (Itself) is (in the "Perfect Practice" of devotionally Me-recognizing and devotionally to-Me-responsive Spiritual Communion with Me) the Process That Realizes the Perfectly Liberating Divine Truth of conditional existence (Which Truth Is Existence Itself).

THREE

When you most directly inspect the conditional self and its objects, all arising conditions (including body, emotions, mind, and the sense of being a defined, separate, and limited self-consciousness) are observed to be mere (apparent) relations of Consciousness (Itself). What is more, Consciousness (Itself), when It is directly "Located" and profoundly Identified With, is not found to be separate, limited, individual, or in any sense un-Happy. And all of the objects, relations, and states that appear to Consciousness (Itself) are, from the "Point of View" of Consciousness (Itself), Inherently (Divinely) Self-Recognized to be transparent (or merely apparent), and un-necessary, and inherently non-binding modifications of Itself.

Therefore, the "consideration" of Consciousness (from the "Point of View" of Consciousness Itself) eventually, inevitably, spontaneously, and most directly (prior to thought, or the mere and conditional knowledge or experience of any object, condition, or state other than Consciousness Itself) Realizes Consciousness (Itself) to be the Transcendental, Inherently Spiritual, Inherently egoless, and Self-Evidently Divine Reality, or the Ultimate Principle in Which egoic (or apparently separate) attention and all conditional experiences are arising. When the Condition of Consciousness Itself is (Thus) Realized, it is Obvious that the Transcendental, Inherently Spiritual, Inherently egoless, and Self-Evidently Divine Self-Condition (and Source-Condition) That <u>Is</u> Being (Itself) is at the root (or Source) of attention—Always Already at the Heart (or Being-Position) of all conscious beings. And, what is more, the objects of functional attention are Realized to be not <u>independent</u> relations of Consciousness Itself, but only transparent

The Liberator (Eleutherios)

(or merely apparent), and un-necessary, and inherently non-binding modifications of That Which Is Consciousness Itself. That is to say, the phenomenal cosmos is, Most Ultimately, Realized to be a Mysterious (or non-mechanical, spontaneous, transparent, or merely apparent, and un-necessary, and inherently non-binding) modification of the Perfectly Subjective Radiance, Inherent Energy, or Self-Existing and Self-Radiant Love-Bliss That is (by Means of the Revelation-Work of My Avatarically Self-Transmitted Divine Spirit-Current) Realized to Be Identical to Consciousness Itself.

FOUR

On the basis of This "radical" (or "at-the-root") "consideration" and Realization, it becomes spontaneously Obvious that there is <u>One</u> Principle—Which <u>Is</u> Self-Existing and Self-Radiant Transcendental, Inherently Spiritual, Inherently egoless, and Self-Evidently Divine Being, Consciousness, and Love-Bliss (or Eternal Happiness)—and not (in Truth, or in Reality) <u>two</u> Principles—which appear to be conditional consciousness (or the faculty of attention, or even an Independent Absolute Consciousness) and (otherwise, or oppositely) everything (or even an Independent All-Pervading "Substance" or Energy) appearing as <u>other</u> than (or object to) that conditional consciousness (or That Independent Absolute Consciousness). Consciousness (Itself) <u>Is</u> the One (Self-Evident, Self-Existing, and Self-Radiant) Principle. It <u>Is</u> (Itself) both Self-Existing Transcendental Divine Being <u>and</u> Self-Radiant Love-Bliss (or Eternal and Inherently Spiritual Happiness). It <u>Is</u> Love-Bliss-"Bright" Being, Unqualifiedly Self-Aware (or Conscious of and <u>As</u> Itself). And there is not anything that can arise as conditional experience (or apparent modification) that is (Really, or in Truth) other than That One, or necessary to That One, or binding to That One.

What you must Realize (or Awaken Into) is the Self-Evident, Self-Existing, and Self-Radiant Consciousness That <u>Is</u> the Real, Ultimate, Transcendental, Non-separate (or Inherently egoless), Inherently Spiritual, and Self-Evidently Divine Self-Condition <u>and</u> Perfectly Subjective Source-Condition of conditional self <u>and</u> of conditional not-self. If That is Realized As the Obvious, then there is <u>Inherent</u> Freedom—and conditional existence (and conditional knowledge, and conditional experience, and even attention itself) has no necessity or binding power.

The Liberator (Eleutherios)

That Realization (Which <u>Is</u> the Realization of Existence Itself) is Realization of the <u>Inherent</u> (and Inherently egoless) Condition (or Divine Self-Condition and Source-Condition) of (apparent) conditional existence. Therefore, That Realization is not—and should not be presumed to be, and, except for the ego-"I" (or separative self-contraction), would not be presumed to be—merely the Goal (or even the Objective Source) of (apparent) conditional existence.

And, when Consciousness (Itself) is Realized most profoundly (or Most Perfectly), apparently arising conditions are inherently non-binding (or become as if transparent, and even non-existent)—Divinely Transfigured, Divinely Transformed, and (Most Ultimately) Divinely Outshined in the One (and Indivisible, and Non-separate, and Indestructible) Transcendental, Inherently Spiritual, Inherently egoless, and Self-Evidently Divine Self-Condition and Source-Condition of all-and-All.

III

Truth, Reality, and Real (Acausal) God

THE LIBERATOR (ELEUTHERIOS)

Truth Is That Which, when "Known" (or fully Realized), Sets you Free. Therefore, Realize Truth (Itself).

Reality Is What <u>Is</u> (no matter what arises or changes or passes away). Therefore, "Locate" (and fully Realize) Reality (Itself).

To "Locate" (and, Thus, to "Know", or fully Realize) Reality (Itself) is to be Set Free. Therefore, Reality (Itself) <u>Is</u> the Divinely Liberating Truth—and to Realize Reality (Itself) is to Realize the Divinely Liberating Truth (and, Thus, to <u>Be</u> Divinely, or Most Perfectly, Free).

Real (Acausal) God Is the Source—or the Source-Condition (and the Non-separate, and Inherently egoless, Self-Condition), and not merely the immediate (or, otherwise, remote), and active (or, otherwise, effective) Cause— of whatever arises, changes, or passes away.

To Find (and, Thus, to "Know", or fully Realize) Real (Acausal) God is to "Know" (or Realize) What <u>Is</u> (or What Remains, or Abides—even as any or all conditions arise or change or pass away). Therefore, to Find (and, Thus, to "Know", or fully Realize) Real (Acausal) God is to "Locate" (and, Thus, to "Know", or fully Realize) Reality (Itself). Indeed, Reality (Itself) <u>Is</u> Real (Acausal) God.

Likewise, to Find (and, Thus, to "Know", or fully Realize) Real (Acausal) God is to be Set Free (even of all bondage, all limitations, and all conditionality of existence). Therefore, to Find (and, Thus, to "Know", or fully Realize) Real (Acausal) God is to "Know" (or fully Realize) Truth (Itself). Indeed, Truth (Itself) <u>Is</u> Real (Acausal) God.

To "Locate" (or fully Realize) Reality (Itself), or to "Know" (or fully Realize) Truth (Itself), is to Find and to Realize Real (Acausal) God.

The Liberator (Eleutherios)

Likewise, to Find (and, Thus, to "Know", or fully Realize) Real (Acausal) God is to "Locate" (or fully Realize) Reality (Itself) and to "Know" (or fully Realize) Truth (Itself).

Indeed, to Find (and, Thus, to "Know", or fully Realize) Real (Acausal) God is to be Liberated from all that is <u>not</u> Real (Acausal) God (or Reality Itself, or Truth Itself).

If Reality (Itself) is "Located" (and, Thus, "Known", or fully Realized), Truth (Itself) is "Known" (or fully Realized)—and you are (Thus and Thereby) Set Free.

In order to "Locate" Reality (Itself), it is necessary to "Locate" What <u>Is</u>—when and where any condition arises, changes, or passes away.

Therefore, it is necessary to always "Locate" the Reality (or Intrinsically Self-Evident Condition) That <u>Remains</u>—while (and even though) any (and every) condition arises, changes, or passes away.

To "Locate" the Reality (or Self-Abiding Condition) That Remains while any particular (or chosen) condition arises, changes, or passes away, it is necessary to <u>Be</u> (or to Stand in the exact Position of) the Reality (or Intrinsically Self-Evident Condition) That Always Already (or Intrinsically) <u>Is</u>—when any (and every) condition arises, changes, or passes away. The Reality (or Intrinsically Self-Evident Condition) That Always Already <u>Is</u> must (necessarily) be <u>Identical</u> to you (As you Always Already <u>Are</u>)—but there <u>Is</u> only One, Intrinsically Self-Evident Condition with Which you are (Inherently, or Always Already) Identical.

<u>What</u> Condition <u>Is</u> yourself—Identical to yourself, and not merely an object to you?

THE LIBERATOR (ELEUTHERIOS)

Only your own Consciousness (or Inherent Tacit Self-Awareness) is Identical (or Perfectly Subjective, and not merely objective) to you.

Therefore, to "Locate" Reality (Itself), and to Realize Truth (Itself), and to be (Thus and Thereby) Set Free, it is only necessary to Self-Abide—<u>As</u> (or in the instant that) your own Consciousness (or Inherent Tacit Self-Awareness) <u>Is</u> Tacitly <u>Self</u>-Aware.

You cannot assume a position <u>relative to</u> your own Consciousness (or Inherent Tacit Self-Awareness) such that your Consciousness (or Inherent Tacit Self-Awareness) can be observed arising, changing, or passing away—because your Consciousness (or Inherent Tacit Self-Awareness) is not an <u>object</u> to you, but It Is the Very "Subject" That <u>Is</u> you.

Real (Acausal) God <u>Is</u> (<u>necessarily</u>) What <u>Is</u>. To Find (or to directly "Locate") your own Consciousness (or your Inherent Tacit Self-Awareness, or your Fundamental, Inherent, and Tacit <u>Self-Apprehension</u> of Conscious Existence) is (<u>necessarily</u>) to Find (or directly "Locate") What <u>Is</u>. Therefore, to Find (or directly "Locate") your own Consciousness (or Inherent Tacit Self-Awareness) is (<u>necessarily</u>) to Find (or directly "Locate") Real (Acausal) God, and to "Locate" Reality (Itself), and to Realize Truth (Itself), and to be (Thus and Thereby) Set Free.

The <u>only</u> Way to Find (and to directly "Know", or fully Realize) Real (Acausal) God, and to "Locate" (and to directly "Know", or fully Realize) Reality (Itself), and to directly "Know" (or fully Realize) Truth (Itself), and to be (Thus and Thereby) Set Most Perfectly Free is the "radical" (or most direct) Process (and Inherently ego-transcending Practice) of "Locating" (or directly Realizing) <u>your</u> <u>own</u>

The Liberator (Eleutherios)

<u>Consciousness</u> (or your Intrinsic and Tacit Self-Awareness, or your Inherent and Tacit Self-Apprehension of Conscious Existence)—because there is <u>no</u> other condition with which you are identical (and that is not otherwise apparently objective to you, and that is not, thus, apparently separate from your own position of direct "Knowledge", or potential Perfect Realization).

To Find Real (Acausal) God, to "Locate" Reality (Itself), to Realize Truth (Itself), and to be (Thus and Thereby) Set Free, you must—by Means of My Graceful Avatarically Given Divine Spiritual Self-Revelation of the Inherently egoless Divine Self-Condition and Person—more and more profoundly Apprehend the Non-separate Self-Condition of Consciousness Itself. As you Thus (by My Avatarically Given Divine Spiritual Grace) profoundly (and more and more profoundly) Apprehend the Self-Evident State, you must (by Means of My Divinely Self-Giving Avataric Spiritual Grace and My Graceful Avatarically Given Divine Self-Revelation) "Locate" and Realize the Divine Source-Condition of all-and-All—Which <u>Is</u> the Divine Self-Condition <u>As</u> Which the Inherent (and Tacit) <u>Self-Apprehension</u> of Conscious Existence is (Itself, and Self-Evidently) Self-Existing.

This practice Awakens in due course (by Means of My Divinely Self-Giving Avataric Spiritual Grace and My Graceful Avatarically Given Divine Self-Revelation), in the case of those who truly practice devotional (and fullest feeling) Communion with My Avatarically-Born bodily (human) Divine Form, My Avatarically Self-Transmitted Spiritual (and Always Blessing) Divine Presence, and My Avatarically Self-Revealed (and Very, and Transcendental, and Perfectly Subjective, and Inherently Spiritual, and Inherently egoless, and Inherently Perfect, and Self-Evidently Divine) State. Indeed, this practice is the most "radical" (or "at-the-root", and Inherently ego-transcending)

THE LIBERATOR (ELEUTHERIOS)

Practice of the only-by-Me Revealed and Given Way of Adidam (or the One and Only by-Me-Revealed and by-Me-Given "Radical" Way of the Heart). It is, even moment to moment, to "Locate" (or Self-Apprehend) your Inherent, Intrinsic, Tacit Self-Awareness of Conscious Existence, and (in that moment to moment practice and process) to perfectly transcend your separate self (or ego-"I", or psycho-physical pattern of self-contraction) in Me (and by Means of heart-Communion with Me)—until I Am Realized (most directly, Most Perfectly, and Absolutely) As the Non-separate Source-Condition and the Inherently egoless Self-Condition of the conditional self-feeling, and As the Non-separate Love-Blissful Source-Condition and the Inherently egoless Love-Blissful Self-Condition of Mere (or Intrinsically Self-Evident) Being (Itself).

The Source-Condition of the Inherent Tacit Self-Awareness of Conscious Existence Is the (Very and Self-Existing and Self-Radiant and Inherently Non-separate and Inherently egoless and Utterly Non-conditional) Tacit Self-Apprehension of Being (Itself).

To Realize the Very (or Inherently Non-separate, Inherently egoless, and Utterly Non-conditional) Tacit Self-Apprehension of Being (Itself) is to Realize Real (Acausal) God, Reality (Itself), Truth (Itself), Freedom (Itself), and Happiness (Itself)—Eternally Most Prior to all conditions, all objects, all separateness, all non-Freedom, and all that is not Real (Acausal) God (or Reality Itself).

And when This Inherently ego-transcending Practice (and Realization) is Itself Most Perfectly Fulfilled, all conditions are (Inherently and spontaneously and always) Divinely Self-Recognized, as transparent to the Very (or Inherently Non-separate, Inherently egoless, and Utterly Non-conditional)

The Liberator (Eleutherios)

Tacit Self-Apprehension of Being (Itself)—and This (Most Ultimately) to the degree of even Most Perfect Indifference, and (at last) to the degree of the Most Perfect Outshining of conditional existence (in the Inherently Perfect, Inherently Non-separate, Inherently egoless, Self-Existing, Self-Radiant, Love-Blissful, and Self-Evidently Divine Self-Condition, and Source-Condition, That <u>Is</u> Mere, or Intrinsically Self-Evident, Being, <u>Itself</u>).

IV

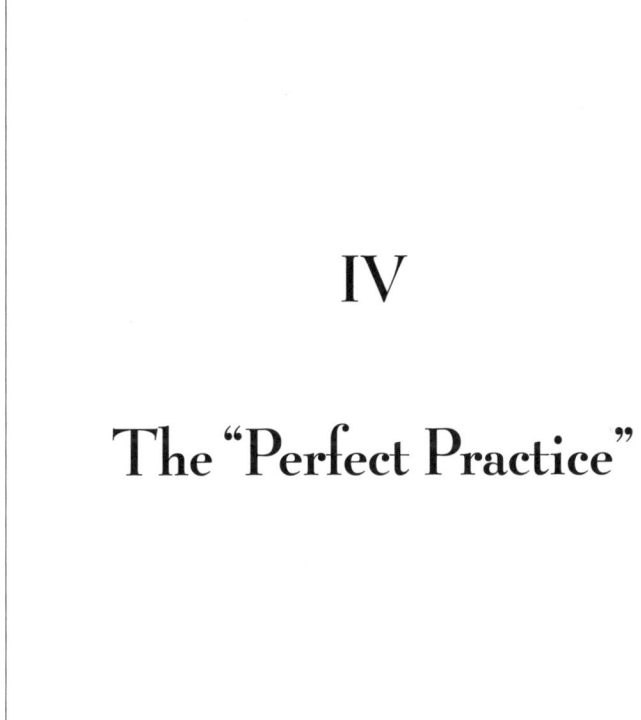

The "Perfect Practice"

THE LIBERATOR (ELEUTHERIOS)

Be Consciousness (Itself).

"Contemplate" Consciousness (Itself).

Transcend everything in Consciousness (Itself).

This is the (Three-Part) "Perfect Practice"—the Epitome of the Ultimate Practice and Process—of the Way of Adidam (Which is the One and Only by-Me-Revealed and by-Me-Given "Radical" Way of the Heart).

ONE

The First Stage (or Part) of the "Perfect Practice" of the only-by-Me Revealed and Given Way of Adidam

Be *Consciousness Itself—Inherently Free (or the Inherently Perfect Witness) in relation to all objects.*

In Reality, "you" (Most Basically, and Non-separately, Prior to the ego-"I", or psycho-physical self-contraction) Are Consciousness (Itself)—Freely (and only apparently) Witnessing and (apparently) being "played upon" (but not actually changed) by body, life-energy, emotion, mind, conditional self-idea, and all relations.

Therefore, the first stage of the "Perfect Practice" of the only-by-Me Revealed and Given Way of Adidam is (as a Stably Realized practice-Disposition) to Be Consciousness (Itself)—or to Stand As (or in the Position of) Consciousness (Itself)—instead of persisting in the conventional and inherently (and, from the "Point of View" of Consciousness Itself, Obviously) un-True presumption that "you" (As Consciousness Itself) are a body-mind (or an always already modified, qualified, limited, defined, and named conditional, or psycho-physical, entity).

To Be (and to Stand As the "Point of View" of) Consciousness (Itself) is not (yet) to Realize What Consciousness (Itself), or Its Ultimate Status, Is—but this first stage (or part) of the "Perfect Practice" of the only-by-Me Revealed and Given Way of Adidam is a matter of Being (or Standing) in the Obvious and (Obviously) Real, Right, and True Disposition (or Inherent Attitude) As Consciousness (Itself) in (apparent) Free association with conditional experience.

THE LIBERATOR (ELEUTHERIOS)

To <u>Be</u> Consciousness (Itself) in (apparent) Free association with (rather than identical to) all that is (apparently) seeming to be the conditional self (or psycho-physical ego-"I") is to Stand <u>As</u> Consciousness—the Free (and Inherently egoless, and Inherently actionless) Witness of the experiential body-mind, and (Thus) no longer mechanically bound by a presumption of <u>conditional identity</u>, in the context of the body-mind.

The body-mind is what "you" (as a matter of convention, and as an experiential presumption) "mean" by the self-reference "I".

Conscious awareness (or attention) <u>as</u> the body-mind is "Narcissus", the separate and separative ego-"I" (or psycho-physical self-contraction)—persisting as if Consciousness (Itself) is <u>identical</u> to Its own (apparent) conditionally arising process of always limited and changing <u>experience</u>.

In the state of egoic identification with the body-mind, attention (and, apparently, Consciousness Itself) is a subject suffering from the absurd presumption that it is identical to its own <u>object</u>.

Consciousness (Itself) is Inherently and Always Already Most Prior to conditional (or psycho-physical) experience.

Consciousness (Itself), Always Already Standing Free (<u>As</u> the Perfectly Prior Witness of conditional experience), and Always Already Standing Free <u>As</u> the Perfectly Prior Witness of the functional observer (or of attention itself), is always already Free of all identification with conditional experience—and, therefore, the (Inherently Perfect) Witness-Consciousness is <u>never</u> an expression, result, or prisoner of conditional experience, conditional knowledge, or conditional existence.

Consciousness (Itself) is Inherently Free of the implications (or effects) of the body-mind and of the apparent cosmos of conditional Nature.

Therefore, the (Inherently Perfect) Witness-Consciousness is not (Itself) un-Happy, afraid, sorrowful, depressed, angry, hungry, lustful, thoughtful, threatened by bodily mortality, or implicated in the alternately pleasurable (or positive) and painful (or negative) states of the body, and of the mind, and (altogether) of conditional Nature.

The (Inherently Perfect) Witness-Consciousness is (in any conditionally arising moment) only <u>apparently</u> associated with the mechanical (or functional) states of the body-mind (and attention) in the realm of conditional Nature.

Therefore, to <u>Be</u> and Stand <u>As</u> Consciousness (Itself), or the Inherently Perfect Witness, in Free (and merely apparent) association with the body-mind and all of conditional Nature (rather than <u>identical</u> to the body-mind in the realm of conditional Nature), is (<u>Inherently</u>) to <u>Be</u> and Stand non-attached (or non-clinging, non-seeking, and non-reacting) to the causes, the effects, the changes, and the apparent present state of the body-mind (and of even all of conditional Nature).

Just so, to (<u>Stably</u>) <u>Be</u> and Stand <u>As</u> Consciousness (Itself), or to <u>Stably</u> Realize the Inherently Perfect Witness, in Free (and merely apparent) association with the body-mind and all of conditional Nature (rather than <u>identical</u> to the body-mind in the realm of conditional Nature), is to (<u>effortlessly</u>, and always already) <u>maintain</u> the Disposition That is <u>inherently</u> non-attached (or non-clinging, non-seeking, and non-reacting) relative to the causes, the effects, the changes, and the apparent present state of the body-mind (and of even all of conditional Nature).

THE LIBERATOR (ELEUTHERIOS)

To (<u>Stably</u>) <u>Be</u> and Stand <u>As</u> Consciousness (Itself), or to <u>Stably</u> Realize the Inherently Perfect Witness, in merely apparent association with every moment of arising conditions, is (Itself) the "Pure" (or Inherently Free) Disposition.

However, the mere affirmation (or self-willed presumption, and willful, or strategic, assertion) of the Witness-Disposition will not <u>cause</u> the body-mind also to achieve and maintain a stable natural state of functional equanimity.

Therefore, in order to (<u>Stably</u>) <u>Be</u> and Stand Freely <u>As</u> Consciousness (Itself), or to Stably Realize the Inherently Perfect Witness, you must, necessarily (by Means of the really counter-egoic sadhana, or right, true, full, and, Spiritually, fully technically responsible practice, of both hearing <u>and</u> seeing devotion to Me), have fully and stably established the natural state of functional psycho-physical equanimity that is (progressively) granted by truly fulfilling the purifying (or, to then, preliminary) process of the developmental stages of the only-by-Me Revealed and Given Way of Adidam (Which is the One and Only by-Me-Revealed and by-Me-Given "Radical" Way of the Heart).

Only such functional equanimity allows (and supports, and indicates) truly and stably free (or functionally un-bound) energy and attention (truly and stably free, in merely apparent association with the body-mind, and even all of conditional Nature)—and thus truly and stably free energy and attention are, together, the essential (and necessary) <u>prerequisite</u> for <u>Stable</u> Realization of the Witness-Position (or Native Attitude) of Consciousness (Itself).

The Liberator (Eleutherios)

Without such free energy and attention (even relative to conditional existence <u>altogether</u>), "you" (as a matter of habitual ego-identification with the experiential patterning of the body-mind) will (inevitably) wander in the patterns (or distractions and preoccupations) associated with the Circle of the body-mind, unable to <u>Stably</u> Stand in the Native Attitude of Consciousness (Itself), even though the Inherently Perfect Witness is the Position in Which "you" (Prior to the ego-"I" of psycho-physical self-contraction) <u>Always</u> <u>Already</u> Exist.

Therefore, practice the ego-surrendering, ego-forgetting, and ego-transcending Way of Adidam, Revealed and Given by Me—until (by Means of My Divinely Self-Giving Avataric Spiritual Grace and My Graceful Avatarically Given Divine Self-Revelation) the signs of the frontal Yoga are (to the degree, and in the manner, necessary in the Way of Adidam) fully developed and fully transcended.

By transcending yourself (or the separate and separative ego-"I" of psycho-physical self-contraction) in the context of the frontal Yoga (such as this Yoga must be engaged by you in the Way of Adidam), be established (by Means of My Divinely Self-Giving Avataric Spiritual Grace and My Graceful Avatarically Given Divine Self-Revelation) in the first stage (or part) of the "Perfect Practice" of the only-by-Me Revealed and Given Way of Adidam—and, Thus (by Means of really counter-egoic devotion to Me, and most profound "Perfect Contemplation" of Me), <u>Stably</u> (and <u>Really</u>, rather than as a mere ego-presumption and illusion) <u>Be</u> and Stand <u>As</u> the Inherently Perfect Witness, Which <u>Is</u> Consciousness (Itself), in Free (and merely apparent) association with all arising conditions and patterns of apparent psycho-physical experience.

THE LIBERATOR (ELEUTHERIOS)

Thus, <u>Stably</u> and <u>Really</u> Standing in the Witness-Position (or Native Attitude) of Consciousness (Itself), Freely (and simply by maintaining every form of functional, practical, relational, and cultural self-discipline you have previously established in the only-by-Me Revealed and Given Way of Adidam) allow the body-mind to persist in a state of balance and ease (or of natural functional equanimity), with energy and attention free of habit-bondage to (and egoic identification with) the patterns of psycho-physical experience.

When all of This has been established, functional energy and attention are free of bondage to the psycho-physical "I" of "Narcissus", and the Inherently Perfect Witness-Consciousness is (once it is Thus and firmly and stably Established) inherently and immediately Free for the second stage of the "Perfect Practice" of the only-by-Me Revealed and Given Way of Adidam.

TWO

The Second Stage (or Part) of the "Perfect Practice" of the only-by-Me Revealed and Given Way of Adidam

"*Contemplate*"—*or, that is to say, <u>directly</u> (or Inherently, and, Thus, Perfectly) <u>Identify with</u>— Consciousness Itself (Most Prior to all objects), until Its Inherently Perfect (Transcendental, Inherently Spiritual, Inherently egoless, and Self-Evidently Divine) Condition becomes Inherently (and Most Perfectly) Obvious.*

Enter into the deep, profound, and most direct heart-Identification with Consciousness Itself, until Its Inherently Perfect "Location", Condition (State, or Self-Nature), and Ultimate Status are Realized.

This is a matter of the Inherent transcending of attention <u>itself</u> (which is the functional essence of the conditional self), and (thus and thereby) of relinquishing <u>all</u> the objects of attention (which are, variously, in the form of ego-idea, mind, emotion, internal life-energy, desire, body, and their relations)—and, in this total event, attention itself is resolved (or dissolved) into its Prior and Inherently Perfect Source-Condition.

This is not a matter of inverting attention upon (and, thus, meditating on) the conditional "I" (or egoic self), in the manner of Narcissus.

This is not a matter of worshipping, inverting upon, meditating on, or egoically identifying with the objective (or, otherwise, apparently Witnessed) inner functional self (or the conditional essence of egoity).

THE LIBERATOR (ELEUTHERIOS)

This is a matter, first of all, of Understanding that the (conditional) essence of the conditional self is not an entity, but it is an <u>activity</u>—the total psycho-physical activity of self-contraction (or, at root, the inherently self-contracted activity that is attention, <u>itself</u>).

Consciousness Itself, apparently associated (and even identified) with functional attention (and, therefore, tending to identify Itself with the functional ego-"I", or the self-contracted totality of body-mind—psycho-physically self-contracted from the apparently threatening field of conditional Nature, and from the Universal, and apparently Independent, Objective Energy That pervades all of conditional Nature), must Understand Itself (or Its own apparent error), and (Thereby, and, Thus, Inherently) Transcend psycho-physical self-contraction (and attention itself)—by Realizing the Inherent (and Obvious, and Inherently Perfect) Condition (or Status) of Consciousness Itself (Which <u>Is</u> Self-Existing and Self-Radiant Transcendental, Inherently Spiritual, Inherently egoless, and Self-Evidently Divine Being and Happiness, or Love-Bliss).

The practice of direct Self-Identification, whereby the Transcendental, Inherently Spiritual, Inherently egoless, and Self-Evidently Divine Self-Condition and Source-Condition That <u>Is</u> Consciousness (Itself) is (Ultimately, Most Perfectly) Realized, may appear, to an external observer (or "outside point of view"), to involve inversion upon the inner conditional and individuated self—but that practice is not, in fact, a process of inversion upon the inner conditional and individuated self.

The Liberator (Eleutherios)

Direct Self-Identification with Consciousness Itself is (as a right, true, full, fully devotional, and profound practice of "Perfect Contemplation") the most direct Means for transcending the ego, or the psycho-physical totality of separate and separative (or self-contracting) conditional self. In the context of the second stage (or part) of the "Perfect Practice" of the only-by-Me Revealed and Given Way of Adidam, right practice of "Perfect Contemplation" is not an effort of functional <u>attention</u>, but it is a Process Prior to functional attention—such that there is direct "Perfect Contemplation" of Consciousness <u>Itself</u> (Which <u>Is</u> the Inherently Perfect Source-Condition in Which attention, and, thus, the individuated and conditional self-consciousness, is presently arising).

Therefore, the process of direct Self-Identification that corresponds to the second stage (or part) of the "Perfect Practice" of the only-by-Me Revealed and Given Way of Adidam is not a matter of the extroversion of attention toward any object, nor is it a matter of the "Narcissistic" introversion of attention upon the subjective interior of the body-mind (or egoic psycho-physical self).

Rather, it is a matter of the yielding (or dissolving) of attention (or conditional self-consciousness) in the Source-Condition from (or in) Which it is presently arising.

It is a matter of Standing <u>As</u> Consciousness Itself (rather than <u>turning attention</u> outward, inward, or toward Consciousness Itself).

THE LIBERATOR (ELEUTHERIOS)

It is a matter of passively allowing attention to settle (or relax, dissolve, and disappear) spontaneously in the Native (or Primal) and Tacit Self-Apprehension of Being (or the Primal Tacit Self-Awareness of Happiness Itself).

Thus, in the moment of the arising of any present object of attention, That Being (Itself), or Consciousness (Itself), to Which (or in Whom) attention and its present object (if any) are arising should be noticed (or Found), entered (or relaxed) into, and (Inherently) Identified with—most profoundly.

This most direct practice is to be engaged in the second stage (or part) of the "Perfect Practice" of the Way of Adidam (or the One and Only by-Me-Revealed and by-Me-Given "Radical" Way of the Heart).

The first stage (or part) of the "Perfect Practice" of the only-by-Me Revealed and Given Way of Adidam is the necessary (and prerequisite) Basis (or Root-Disposition) in Which the second stage (or part) of the "Perfect Practice" of the only-by-Me Revealed and Given Way of Adidam is to be engaged.

The second stage (or part) of the "Perfect Practice" of the only-by-Me Revealed and Given Way of Adidam is the Process in Which attention is relaxed, forgotten, and disappeared in the Native Seat (or heart-root) of Happiness (or Love-Bliss-Fullness) Itself, until the Perfectly Subjective Space of Consciousness (Itself), or the Perfectly Subjective (and Tacit) Self-Apprehension of Being (Itself), becomes Obvious—Beyond (or Most Prior to) the heart-focus.

The Liberator (Eleutherios)

The characteristic exercise associated with the second stage (or part) of the "Perfect Practice" of the only-by-Me Revealed and Given Way of Adidam is that of persistent attention-transcending devotional "gazing" into (or by-Me-devotionally-heart-Attracted, and to-Me-devotionally-heart-responsive, mere tacit observing of) the region of the right side of the heart—which region is the functional seat (or root-place) of the origin (or first arising) of attention itself, and which region is also (Prior to the knot of attention, or the root-feeling of relatedness) the Native Seat and Place of Origin (and the Doorway to the Most Prior Space) of My Avatarically Self-Transmitted Divine Spirit-Current of Love-Bliss Itself.

This attention-transcending devotional "gazing" (or devotional exercise of mere tacit observing) is to be engaged such and so that attention itself (free of distraction by the outgoing motives associated with the body-mind) may be relaxed and relinquished There, in the right side of the heart—and, Thus and Thereby, forgotten (or disappeared) in the Primal (and Tacit) Self-Apprehension of Being (Itself), or of Love-Bliss (Itself), "Located" (or to be Realized) There.

This attention-transcending devotional "gazing" (or devotional exercise of mere tacit observing) is made effective (and possible) by the relaxing of attention into the Inherent Attractiveness of My Avataric Spiritual Transmission of the Self-Evidently Divine Love-Bliss-Current of Being (Itself)—Avatarically Self-Revealed (and Spiritually Self-Transmitted) by Me (and <u>As</u> Me), at Its heart-root (or Perfectly Subjective Point of Origin), in the right side of the heart.

THE LIBERATOR (ELEUTHERIOS)

The bodily root (or Origin, or Original Space) of the Tacit Self-Apprehension of Being (Itself) is Inherently "Located" (and is, by Means of My Avatarically Self-Transmitted Divine Spiritual Grace, to be Found) in the right side of the heart—As the Tangible Divine Spirit-Current of profound, constant, Original, Uncaused, and Non-conditional Happiness (or Love-Bliss).

The Divine Spirit-Current of Love-Bliss is Transmitted, Revealed, Intensified, and made Attractive by (and As) Me—and (by Means of My Divinely Self-Giving Avataric Spiritual Grace and My Graceful Avatarically Given Divine Self-Revelation) It is to be Received, through your (heart-responsively) ego-transcending "Perfect Contemplation" of My Avatarically-Born bodily (human) Divine Form, My Avatarically Self-Transmitted Spiritual (and Always Blessing) Divine Presence, and My Avatarically Self-Revealed (and Very, and Transcendental, and Perfectly Subjective, and Inherently Spiritual, and Inherently egoless, and Inherently Perfect, and Self-Evidently Divine) State.

My Divine Spirit-Current of Love-Bliss (Thus Avatarically Transmitted, Revealed, Intensified, made Attractive, and Received) Draws you (in the course of your "Perfect Practice" of the only-by-Me Revealed and Given Way of Adidam) into (and, Ultimately, Beyond) the right side of the heart, and (Thereby) Reveals the heart-root of Consciousness (Itself)—after the earlier (or pre-"Perfect Practice") developmental stages of right, true, full, and fully devotional practice of the Way of Adidam have been fulfilled and matured, and (thus and thereby) the necessary (and prerequisite) processes of thorough self-observation, most fundamental self-Understanding, really ego-transcending devotion to Me, and fully technically responsible Spiritual Communion with Me have (by Means of My Divinely Self-Giving Avataric

The Liberator (Eleutherios)

Spiritual Grace and My Graceful Avatarically Given Divine Self-Revelation) progressively established the necessary signs associated with maturity in the only-by-Me Revealed and Given Way of Adidam in the really ego-transcending devotional and Spiritual context of the frontal Yoga.

When (by Means of My Divinely Self-Giving Avataric Spiritual Grace and My Graceful Avatarically Given Divine Self-Revelation) practice of the only-by-Me Revealed and Given Way of Adidam becomes profound Self-Identification with the Inherent (and Tacit) Self-Apprehension of Being (Which Is Consciousness Itself—Most Prior to self-contraction, Most Prior to the body-mind, Most Prior to any objective referents, and Most Prior to the root-feeling of relatedness), the Inherently Free State of Consciousness (Itself) Is Spontaneously Revealed and Enjoyed.

Likewise, by Means of My Divinely Self-Giving Avataric Spiritual Grace and My Graceful Avatarically Given Divine Self-Revelation, the Divine Status of Consciousness (Itself) Is (in due course) Revealed, and (Thus and Thereby) Realized to Be (Most Perfectly) Obviously So.

Consciousness (Itself) Is Self-Existing Transcendental (Inherently egoless and Self-Evidently Divine) Being and Eternal Love-Bliss (or Self-Radiant and Inherently Spiritual Happiness).

When This Divine (and Inherently egoless) Self-Condition (of Consciousness, Itself) Is Most Perfectly (Fully, Stably, and Most "Brightly", or Love-Bliss-Fully) Obvious, the third stage (or part) of the "Perfect Practice" of the only-by-Me Revealed and Given Way of Adidam has (spontaneously, and only and entirely by Means of My Divinely Self-Giving Avataric Spiritual Grace and My Graceful Avatarically Given Divine Self-Revelation) begun.

THREE

The Third Stage (or Part) of the "Perfect Practice" of the only-by-Me Revealed and Given Way of Adidam

Self-Abide As Inherently Perfect Consciousness Itself, Inherently Transcending (but not strategically excluding or seeking) any or all objects—and, Thus, Tacitly Divinely Self-Recognize all objects in and As Self-Existing and Self-Radiant (Transcendental, Inherently Spiritual, Inherently egoless, and Self-Evidently Divine) Being, Consciousness, Love-Bliss, or Happiness, until all objects are Outshined in That.

Consciousness Itself (or Inherent Being) is Transcendentally Existing, Most Prior to attention in the apparent cosmic realm of conditional Nature.

Transcendental, Inherently Spiritual, Inherently egoless, and Self-Evidently Divine Consciousness Is Inherently Perfect Reality, or the Source-Condition of attention, and of the presumption of separate self, and of the total body-mind, and of even all of conditional Nature (including the Universal, or All-Pervading and apparently Objective, Energy of Which all the objects, conditions, states, and presumed-to-be-separate individuals in the realm of conditional Nature are apparently composed).

When Transcendental, Inherently Spiritual, Inherently egoless, and Self-Evidently Divine Consciousness (or the Inherent and Tacit Self-Apprehension of Being, Itself) is (by Means of My Divinely Self-Giving Avataric Spiritual Grace and My Graceful Avatarically Given Divine Self-Revelation)

The Liberator (Eleutherios)

Awakened As the Real Self-Condition (the Indefinable Identity, or Infinite Source-Condition, of functional attention), then the ego-"I" (or the self-contraction, or the ego-possessed body-mind) is directly and inherently transcended, and the Inherent Condition (or the Inherently Perfect Source-Condition) of conditional Nature is Revealed As the Obvious, even in all the apparent moments of spontaneous functional attention to the apparent conditions and relations of the apparent body-mind.

Such Obviousness is the Primary Characteristic of the only-by-Me Revealed and Given Awakening to the Divinely Enlightened seventh stage of life—and only That Awakening manifests (or Demonstrates Itself) as the capability for "Practicing" and fulfilling the third stage (or part) of the "Perfect Practice", Which is the Most Ultimate and Most Perfect Form of the Way of Adidam (or the One and Only by-Me-Revealed and by-Me-Given "Radical" Way of the Heart).

Therefore, when (by Means of My Divinely Self-Giving Avataric Spiritual Grace and My Graceful Avatarically Given Divine Self-Revelation) Self-Identification with (Transcendental, Inherently Spiritual, Inherently egoless, and Self-Evidently Divine) Consciousness (Itself), or the Tacit Self-Apprehension of Being (Itself), is complete (tacit, uncaused, and undisturbed), simply Self-Abide As That and allow all conditions (or all of conditional Nature) to arise (and to change, and to pass away, or even to never arise at all) in the Self-Radiance and Perfectly Subjective Space of (Self-Existing, Transcendental, Non-separate, Inherently Spiritual, Inherently egoless, Indivisible, Indestructible, Inherently Spiritually "Bright", or Love-Bliss-Full, and Self-Evidently Divine) Being (Itself), or Consciousness (Itself).

THE LIBERATOR (ELEUTHERIOS)

As conditions arise in That "Open-Eyed" (or Self-Existing and Self-Radiant) Consciousness, they are Divinely Self-Recognized (and inherently transcended) as transparent (or merely apparent), and un-necessary, and inherently non-binding modifications of Consciousness Itself.

Self-Abide Thus. Divinely Self-Recognize Thus. Let actions arise spontaneously, in and via the Inherent (and Inherently Spiritual) Love-Bliss of Self-Radiant and Self-Existing Transcendental Divine Being—until all apparent conditions and relations of the apparent body-mind are Divinely Transfigured, Divinely Transformed, and (Most Ultimately, and at last) Divinely Translated (or Outshined in the Self-Existing and Self-Radiant Transcendental, Inherently Spiritual, Inherently egoless, and Self-Evidently Divine Self-Condition of Being, Itself—Which Is the Heart, the Perfectly Subjective Source-Condition, and the Spiritually "Bright" Free Sphere and Self-Domain of all conditional beings).

This Most Ultimate Form of the "Perfect Practice" is the Most Ultimate Form of the only-by-Me Revealed and Given practice of the only-by-Me Revealed and Given Way of Adidam.

This Most Ultimate Realization is the only-by-Me Realized Basis (or Source-Position and Self-Position) from Which all of the Teachings and every discipline associated with the only-by-Me Revealed and Given Way of Adidam have been Revealed and Given by Me.

Therefore, This Revelation-Teaching is an Epitome (or Simplest Statement) of all that I am here to Say to you about the Most Ultimate and Most Perfect Realization of Reality, Truth, Happiness, Love-Bliss-"Brightness", or Real (Acausal) God.

V

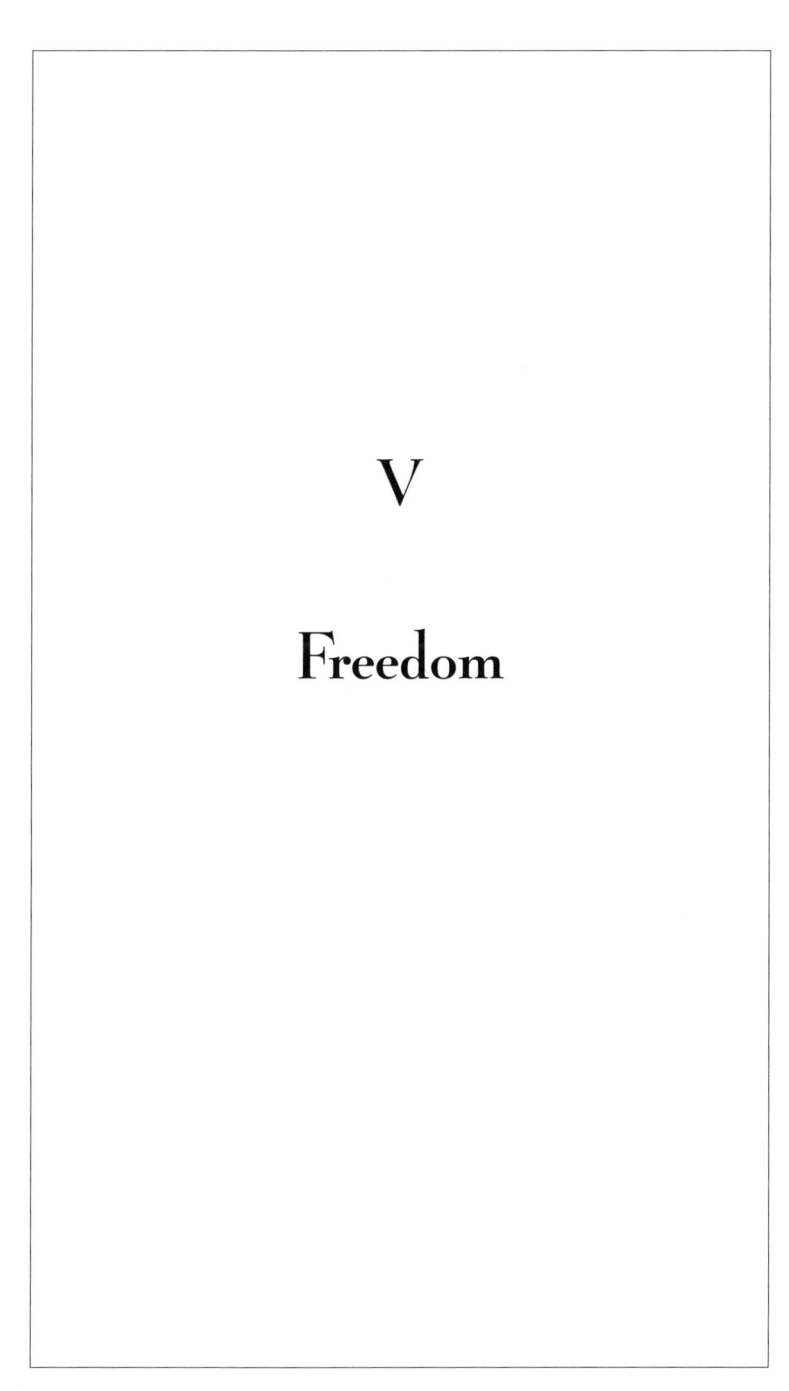

Freedom

THE LIBERATOR (ELEUTHERIOS)

ONE

The conventions of human life and civilization are based on the mechanical, arbitrary, and uninspected identification of Consciousness (Itself) with the patterns of conditional experience. Thus, human pursuits are (as a matter of convention and habit) directed toward self-centered elaboration of conditional experience, self-fulfillment via conditional experience, and strategic escape within (or from) the context of conditional experience. Both conventional science and conventional religion are conventions of egoity in the embrace and pursuit and avoidance of conditional experience. All conventional human pursuits are a bewildered search, founded on uninspected egoic identification with conditional experience, rather than "radically" direct Self-Identification with the Inherent Love-Bliss-Happiness of Consciousness Itself, or Self-Existing and Self-Radiant Transcendental, Inherently Spiritual, Inherently egoless, and Self-Evidently Divine Being (Itself). Thus, either conditional experience or conditional Nature or materiality or "God" (as the "Reality" That is presumed to Exist entirely Exclusively, as "Other" than, and as "Other" to, the conditional self and conditional Nature) tends to be presumed and propagandized as the First, the Ultimate, the One, or the Most Important Principle—but such presumptions are simply the ultimate illusions, or deluded visions, that are developed from the base of the ego (or Consciousness presumed to be limited to and bound by conditional, or psycho-physical, experiencing).

If (or when) you are My truly mature devotee, Free to be Supremely Intelligent, and Ready to Truly and Fully Embrace the "Perfect Practice" of Truth and Happiness, then your practice of the only-by-Me Revealed and Given Way of Adidam (Which is the One and Only by-Me-Revealed

and by-Me-Given "Radical" Way of the Heart) becomes most direct and profound Self-Identification with Consciousness (Itself), or the Inherent (and Tacit) Self-Apprehension of Being (Itself)—Prior to all doubt, Prior to any limitation by conditional experience, Prior to all "looking" at objects (within or without, high or low, positive or negative), and Prior to any qualification (or limitation) by the root-feeling of relatedness itself. When This Self-Identification is Inherently Most Perfect and Complete, such that It is not dependent on any act or state of attention, or of mind, or of emotion, or of desire, or of life-energy, or of body, or of conditional Nature itself, then all conditional experience (or the total realm of conditional Nature, and of psycho-physical egoity) is Inherently and Tacitly (Divinely) Self-Recognized in That (or as a transparent, or merely apparent, and un-necessary, and inherently non-binding modification of Self-Existing and Self-Radiant Transcendental, Inherently Spiritual, Inherently egoless, and Self-Evidently Divine Being). When This Divinely Enlightened (or Me-"Bright") Disposition is Awake, the "Perfect Practice" of My devotee is simply to Self-Abide in and <u>As</u> the Self-Existing and Self-Radiant Divine Self-Condition of Being (Itself), Inherently Transcending all conditions—but Divinely Self-Recognizing and allowing them, rather than resisting and excluding them. And the inevitable persistence in This Self-Existing and Self-Radiant Identity and This Inherent and spontaneous (and Inherently egoless, and Self-Evidently Divine) Self-Recognition Divinely Transfigures, Divinely Transforms, and (Most Ultimately, and at last) Divinely Outshines the body-mind and all conditional worlds, in the "Practicing" course of the only-by-Me Revealed and Given seventh stage of life in the Way of Adidam (Which "Practice" is also otherwise Named by Me "Ati-Ruchira Yoga", or "the Yoga of the All-Outshining 'Brightness'").
In the meantime (until the spontaneous Demonstration of Divine Translation, or of all-and-All-Outshining "Brightness"),

THE LIBERATOR (ELEUTHERIOS)

there is simple Self-Abiding, in and <u>As</u> the Self-Existing and Self-Radiant Love-Bliss of Transcendental, Inherently Spiritual, Inherently egoless, and Self-Evidently Divine Being—and such Divine Self-Abiding spontaneously expresses Itself as Radiance, Happiness, Love-Bliss, Blessing, and Love-Help in all relations.

TWO

The Ultimate Wisdom Inherently Understands, Transcends, and Stands Free of the life-drama. Happiness (Itself)—Which <u>Is</u> Transcendental, Inherently Spiritual, Inherently egoless, and Self-Evidently Divine Consciousness (Itself), or Being (Itself)—Inherently Transcends the confrontation between the ego-"I" and the patterns of conditional Nature.

Every ego-"I" (or ego-possessed body-mind) is involved in a passionate and mortal struggle with the Force and the forces and the parts and the patterns of conditional Nature.

Every ego-"I" is active as the opponent of all opponents, but there is no Final Victory—and every opposition is an irrational (or fruitless) search for Equanimity, Peace, and Love-Bliss.

Every ego-"I" always tends to desire and seek an ego-made refuge from irrational opponents. That strategy of self-preservation is entertained in temporary pleasures and solitary places, but it is not finally attained. Only the ego-"I" (the separate and separative body-mind) is opposed and opposing—and every opposition is an irrational (or fruitless) search for Freedom.

The ego-"I" is inherently, always, and irrationally (or meaninglessly) opposed. The "other" is always an opponent (in effect, if not by intention). The ego-"I" is confronted only by binding forces, and it is itself a force that is tending to bind every "other". The "other" and the ego-"I" are mad relations, always together in the growling pit, bound by conditional Nature to do such Nature's deeds to one another. And, as conditional experience increases, it begins to become obvious (to the conditional knower of conditional experience) that conditional Nature itself is an Immense Pattern that always seeks (and inevitably attains) superiority, dominance, and destruction of every conditional part and every conditional self.

The Great Exclusive "Other"—whether "It" is called "Nature" or "Nature's 'God'"—is your egoically presumed Opponent (or "That" with "Which" the ego-"I" is only, and necessarily, struggling—and toward "Which" the ego-"I" is merely seeking). Therefore, the Great Exclusive "Other" is not your Refuge (or That in Which there is Inherent Freedom from egoity itself). And the very perception and conception of "difference" (or of "otherness", or of the Great Exclusive "Other") is the sign that the separate (and inherently separative) ego-"I" (or psycho-physical self-contraction), rather than Truth (Itself), is the presumed basis of apparent (or conditional) existence.

Truth is Most Prior (or Eternal) Freedom and Humor—whether or not the "Other" (or the Opponent) seems to be present. Therefore, Truth is the Only Perfect Refuge. And if you surrender to the Truth—Which Is Transcendental, Inherently Spiritual, Inherently egoless, and Self-Evidently Divine Being (Itself), Consciousness (Itself), or Inherent Happiness (Itself), the Ultimate (and Perfectly Subjective) Source of the conditional self and all that is objective to it—then there is an Awakening from this nightmare of condemned life and its passionate search for pleasure, strategic escape, Final Victory, and Freedom Itself.

When the heart-response (or Awakening) to Truth is Real, then the frightened and self-bound motive toward the world (and the inevitable round of pleasures, confrontations, doubts, searches, and always temporary releases) begins to fall away. The mortal self becomes simpler in action, more

The Liberator (Eleutherios)

free of habitual reactions to insult and frustration of purpose, more humorous in the face of conditional Nature and all the fools of conditional Nature, more compassionate, and inclined to selfless (or sorrowless) Love. The ego-"I" that is Awakening Beyond itself is inclined to set others free of itself, rather than to bind them to itself, or to themselves, or to one another. The ego-"I" that is nearly dissolved is more often solitary, more deeply renounced, without cares or motivations or doubts or angry despair of conditional self or conditional others. At last—when the self-contraction is (by Inherently egoless "Practice") Inherently (and Most Perfectly) surrendered, forgotten, and transcended in its Most Prior Condition (of Transcendental, Inherently Spiritual, Inherently egoless, and Self-Evidently Divine Being)—all of this arising of body-mind and world is Divinely Self-Recognized to be an unnecessary and superficial dream, a stressful inclination that is (suddenly) Outshined in the Most Prior and Self-Radiant Happiness of Divine Self-Existence.

The usable Lesson of a difficult life proves that you must (thoroughly) observe, (most fundamentally) Understand, and (Most Perfectly) transcend your own conditional personality and destiny. Every individual is only seeking not to be destroyed. Therefore, Understand and become more tolerant of others. Cease to struggle with others and yourself. Do not become bound up in the usual search for dominance, consolation, pleasure, and release. There is neither Final Release nor Ultimate Happiness in the objective (or "outside") or the subjective (or "inside") realms of merely conditional existence.

Observe and Understand the theatre of ego-"I". Learn to be free of the reactivity and seeking that characterize the conditional self-principle (which is only the self-contracting body-mind in confrontation with the apparent realm of conditional Nature). Thus, allow functional energy and attention to be free of the motive toward the body-mind and its relations. Let functional energy and attention be free (instead) to transcend this conditionally arising world-theatre (or mummery of limitations), and, Thus (by Means of My Divinely Self-Giving Avataric Spiritual Grace and My Graceful Avatarically Given Divine Self-Revelation), to Self-Abide in the Divine "Bright" Spherical Self-Domain That is at the Origin of conditional self-consciousness. Then, if the body-mind and all of conditional Nature arise, see all of it from the Original Position of Transcendental, Inherently Spiritual, Inherently egoless, and Self-Evidently Divine Self-Consciousness. See that conditional self and conditional Nature are a transparent (or merely apparent), and un-necessary, and inherently non-binding modification of the Self-Existing Self-Radiance (or Inherently Free "Bright" Love-Bliss-Energy) of Consciousness (Itself), Which Is Self-Existing, and Self-Radiant, and Inherently egoless, and Self-Evidently Divine Being (Itself).

THREE

"Consider" all of this, and, by Means of right, true, and full devotional practice of the only-by-Me Revealed and Given Way of Adidam (Which is the One and Only by-Me-Revealed and by-Me-Given "Radical" Way of the Heart), allow attention to be released from the dilemma and the search associated with the body-mind, high or low in the realm of conditional Nature. In the (progressive) context of the stages of practice previous to the "Perfect Practice" of the Way of Adidam, surrender the body-mind to Me in daily life and meditation—until the total body-mind accepts (or freely and easily demonstrates) the constant discipline (and inherently motiveless attitude) of equanimity. By Means of My Divinely Self-Giving Avataric Spiritual Grace and My Graceful Avatarically Given Divine Self-Revelation, Real and Stable Self-Identification with the Witness-Position and Native Attitude (or Prior Disposition) of Consciousness Itself (in the manner of the first stage, or part, of the "Perfect Practice" of the only-by-Me Revealed and Given Way of Adidam) will, in due course, <u>spontaneously</u> occur. Likewise, when (by Means of My Divinely Self-Giving Avataric Spiritual Grace and My Graceful Avatarically Given Divine Self-Revelation) the seeking effort of binding want and need relative to the motives and states of the body-mind has come to rest in the Witness-Position and Native Attitude (or Prior Disposition) of Consciousness (Itself), the second stage (or part) of the "Perfect Practice" of the Way of Adidam has the necessary Basis to begin.

In the second stage (or part) of the "Perfect Practice" of the only-by-Me Revealed and Given Way of Adidam, let attention be dissolved in the Heart-Space of Being, Self-Revealed by Me (and <u>As</u> Me) in (and Prior to, and Beyond) the right side of the heart. Thus, transcend attention, and every conditionally arising object—by Means of the Searchless (or Inherently egoless) Exercise (or Inherent and Tacit Self-Apprehension) of Being (Itself). Thus, directly "Locate" the Perfectly (or Most Priorly) Subjective Space That Is Consciousness Itself—Prior to psycho-physical self-consciousness. Thus, transcend attention by Standing As Consciousness Itself—in and As the Heart-Space of Being (Itself).

Therefore, in the context of the second stage (or part) of the "Perfect Practice" of the only-by-Me Revealed and Given Way of Adidam, do not merely "look" at (or strategically turn attention to) the heart-root of attention. The heart-root that is thus "seen" is merely another object of attention. And the "looking" is (itself) merely another exercise of the seeking-motive of attention (and of self-contraction) itself. Therefore, such "looking" is merely another experience of the knot that blocks the Doorway to My Avatarically Self-Transmitted Divine Spirit-Current and Space of Divine Love-Bliss, in and Beyond the right side of the heart.

In the context of the second stage (or part) of the "Perfect Practice" of the only-by-Me Revealed and Given Way of Adidam, do not "look" at the heart-root of attention, but always directly transcend attention itself (and the knot that blocks the Doorway in the right side of the heart). Do This by Means of heart-Attracted devotional response to Me.

I Always Already Stand Most Perfectly Beyond and Prior to the knot in the right side of the heart. Therefore, in the second stage (or part) of the "Perfect Practice" of the only-by-Me Revealed and Given Way of Adidam, "Locate" Me (by Means of My Divinely Self-Giving Avataric Spiritual Grace and My Graceful Avatarically Given Divine Self-Revelation), always immediately and effortlessly, via (and <u>As</u>) My Avataric Spiritual Self-Transmission of the Self-Evidently Divine Love-Bliss-Current of Being—and then (and Thus, and Thereby), self-forgotten in <u>Me</u>, simply <u>Be</u> the Mere and Tacit and Inherently Self-Apprehending Spirit-Current of Being (Itself). In This Manner, "Locate" and <u>Be</u> Consciousness Itself, Most Prior to any object or any point of attention. <u>Thus</u>, <u>Be</u> Consciousness Itself, Love-Bliss Itself, or Being Itself, Most Prior to objects—until the Most Prior State (and Ultimate Status) of Consciousness (Itself) Is (by Means of My Divinely Self-Giving Avataric Spiritual Grace and My Graceful Avatarically Given Divine Self-Revelation) Obvious, beyond any possibility of doubt.

In the "Perfect Practice" of the only-by-Me Revealed and Given Way of Adidam, the Purpose of "Locating" the Inherent Love-Bliss-Apprehension of Being (via My Avatarically Self-Transmitted Divine Spirit-Current of Love-Bliss— Revealed by Me, and <u>As</u> Me, in the right side of the heart) is to transcend attention in its Perfectly <u>Subjective</u> root. The Locus That is Revealed in the right side of the heart is the <u>bodily</u> root of attention (or the bodily Doorway to the Source-Condition of body, mind, and attention, Which Divine Source-Condition Is Non-conditional Love-Bliss-Happiness). The brain, the abdominal region, and every other extended part of the body, including the middle station and the left side of the heart, are merely bodily <u>objects</u> of attention (or extensions of mind or life-energy, at a distance from the heart-root), and mere <u>attention</u> to any one of them is itself an involvement in a motion of mind or life-energy that leads to all kinds of gross and subtle objects.

Therefore, in the context of the second stage (or part) of the "Perfect Practice" of the only-by-Me Revealed and Given Way of Adidam, persistently "Locate" the Inherent

THE LIBERATOR (ELEUTHERIOS)

(and Tacit) Self-Apprehension of Being (Itself), by devotionally "falling" into My Avatarically Self-Transmitted Divine Spirit-Current of Love-Bliss (or Primal Happiness) in the right side of the heart. Do not merely "look" at the objective heart-root, but (by Means of My Divinely Self-Giving Avataric Spiritual Grace and My Graceful Avatarically Given Divine Self-Revelation, in the context of Inherently ego-transcending "Perfect Contemplation" of Me) Be at (and via, and Most Prior to) the heart-root. Thus, transcend every object (and even the root-feeling of relatedness itself) in the Transcendental (and Inherently Perfect) "Subject" (or Consciousness Itself)—by "Locating" the Primal Love-Bliss-Happiness apparently associated with (but Always Already Free-Standing, Most Prior to) the right side of the heart. Thus, "Locate" the Non-separate Love-Bliss-Current of Merely Being. Thus, "Contemplate" Merely Being—Identical to Self-Existing (or Non-conditional, and Non-caused), and (altogether) Self-Radiant and Un-qualified, Consciousness Itself. Thus, "Contemplate" Being-Awareness. Thus, "Contemplate" Fundamental, Non-caused, and (altogether) Self-Existing, Self-Radiant, and Non-conditional Love-Bliss-Happiness. "Contemplate" Thus, until it becomes Obvious that Consciousness (Itself), As Love-Bliss-Being (Itself), has no objects, or knowledge, or limitations at all. In due course, on the Basis of the most profound devotional and Spiritual exercise of the second stage (or part) of the "Perfect Practice" of the only-by-Me Revealed and Given Way of Adidam (and only and entirely by Means of My Divinely Self-Giving Avataric Spiritual Grace and My Graceful Avatarically Given Divine Self-Revelation), the third stage (or part) of the "Perfect Practice" of the only-by-Me Revealed and Given Way of Adidam will be Awakened, spontaneously—such that, when objects (apparently) return, "you" (As Inherently egoless, Non-separate Consciousness Itself) will Tacitly (Divinely) Self-Recognize them as (merely) apparent projections in (and merely apparent modifications of) That Self-Existing and Self-Radiant Love-Bliss-Space That is Wholly, Transcendentally, Perfectly, and (Self-Evidently) Divinely Subjective—Rooted in (and Identical to) Being (Itself), or (Only) Consciousness (Itself).

In the third stage (or part) of the "Perfect Practice" (which is the only-by-Me Revealed and Given seventh stage of life in the only-by-Me Revealed and Given Way of Adidam), the countless objects of conditional Nature (and the root-feeling of relatedness associated with all forms of conditional Nature, or all conditional appearances) are perceived and cognized and Divinely Self-Recognized in the Self-Existing and Self-Radiant Space of (Inherently egoless and Self-Evidently Divine) Consciousness (Itself), or (Inherently egoless and Self-Evidently Divine) Being (Itself)—but there is no loss of Transcendental, and Inherently Spiritual (or Love-Blissful), and Inherently egoless, and Self-Evidently Divine Self-Consciousness, Most Prior Freedom, and Inherently Perfect Happiness.

FOUR

Be Consciousness (Itself).

This foundation stage (or prerequisite part) of the "Perfect Practice" of the only-by-Me Revealed and Given Way of Adidam is associated with a natural (or effortless) state of functional psycho-physical equanimity—such that functional energy and attention are free to dissolve (or be forgotten) in the by-Me-Revealed "Perfect Space" of Being (Itself), or Love-Bliss-Consciousness (Itself).

"Contemplate" Consciousness (Itself).

This middle stage (or intensively deepening counter-egoic exercise, and, thus, central part) of the "Perfect Practice" of the only-by-Me Revealed and Given Way of Adidam is complete when there is no longer the slightest feeling (or possibility) of doubt relative to the Divine Status of Consciousness (Itself)—As the Transcendental, and Inherently Spiritual (or Love-Blissful), and Inherently egoless, and Self-Evidently Divine, and Perfectly Subjective Source (and Source-Condition) of the conditional self and of all of conditional Nature.

Transcend everything in Consciousness (Itself).

The fundamental characteristic of this final stage (or inherently egoless, and Truly Most Perfect part) of the "Perfect Practice" of the only-by-Me Revealed and Given Way of Adidam is that there is no longer any ego-binding identification with the arising of functional attention, and no longer any ego-binding identification with any form of conditional self or conditional world—and this final stage (or part) of the

The Liberator (Eleutherios)

"Perfect Practice" of the only-by-Me Revealed and Given Way of Adidam is complete (or most finally, and Most Perfectly, Demonstrated) when the totality of all (apparently) arising objects and limited (and limiting) conditions (and the root-feeling of relatedness itself, and even all of "difference") is Utterly Outshined By and In (and, Thus, Divinely Translated Into) My Avatarically Self-Revealed Love-Bliss-"Bright" Divine Self-Condition (and Divine "Bright" Spherical Self-Domain) of Perfectly Subjective (or Transcendental, Inherently Spiritual, Inherently egoless, and Self-Evidently Divine) Self-Existence.

FIVE

Recognize Me
>   With your heart's devotion,
>   and
>   (Thus and Thereby)
>   Accept The Freedom and The Happiness
>   That Are Inherent In Existence Itself.

Respond to Me
>   With your heart's devotion,
>   and
>   (Thus and Thereby)
>   Transcend the feeling of relatedness
>   In The Tacit Self-Apprehension Of Being (Itself).

"Contemplate" Me
>   With your heart's devotion,
>   and
>   (Thus and Thereby)
>   Be Conscious
>   <u>As</u> The Non-Separate and Tacitly Self-Apprehending
>   Spiritual Current Of Being (Itself).

I <u>Am</u> Self-Existing
>   <u>As</u> Consciousness (Itself),
>   Which <u>Is</u> Self-Radiant
>   <u>As</u> Love-Bliss-Happiness
>   and
>   Infinite and Eternal Freedom.

Consciousness (Itself) <u>Is</u>
>   Self-Existing
>   and Self-Radiant
>   Transcendental,
>   and Inherently Spiritual,
>   (or Inherently Love-Bliss-Full),
>   and Inherently egoless,
>   and Self-Evidently Divine
>   Being (Itself).

The Liberator (Eleutherios)

Freedom,
   or Consciousness (Itself),
   <u>Is</u>
   Inherent Happiness,
   "Bright" Self-Radiance,
   or Un-limited Love-Bliss
   —Not self-contraction,
   separateness,
   separativeness,
   and "difference".
The Un-limited Love-Bliss-Fullness
   Of Transcendental,
   and Inherently Spiritual
   (or Inherently Love-Bliss-Full),
   and Inherently egoless,
   and Self-Evidently Divine Being
   Spontaneously Demonstrates Itself
   Most Perfectly,
   As Self-Abiding Divine Self-Recognition
   Of the total body-mind
   and the totality of conditional worlds,
   In The Un-limited Love-Bliss-Radiance
   Of Transcendental,
   and Inherently Spiritual
   (or Inherently Love-Bliss-Full),
   and Inherently egoless,
   and Self-Evidently Divine Being,
   Until The Cosmic Vast
   Of body-mind and conditional worlds
   Is Outshined
   By That Divine Self-"Brightness",
   and
   (Thus)
   Divinely Translated
   Into The Condition and The Domain
   Of That Divine Self-"Brightness".

THE LIBERATOR (ELEUTHERIOS)

This Is The Heart-Word Of Eleutherios,
    The Divine Liberator,
    The Inherently egoless Acausal Personal Presence
    Of Reality and Truth
    (The all-and-All-Liberating
    Self-Condition and Source-Condition
    Of all-and-All,
    Which <u>Is</u> The Only and Acausal <u>Real</u> God
    Of all-and-All),
    here Appearing
    As The Ruchira Avatar,
    The Avataric Incarnation Of The "Bright",
    Adi Da Samraj—
    Who <u>Is</u> Da,
    The Source, The "Substance", The Gift, The Giver,
    and
    The Very Person
    Of
    The One and Only "Bright" Divine Love-Bliss,
    Which <u>Is</u> Eleutherios,
    The Divine Liberator
    Of
    all-and-All.

The Liberator (Eleutherios)

This Is The Heart-Blessing Word Of Eleutherios,
   The Divine Liberator,
   The Inherently egoless Acausal Personal Presence
   Of Reality and Truth
   (The all-and-All-Liberating
   Self-Condition and Source-Condition
   Of all-and-All,
   Which <u>Is</u> The Only and Acausal <u>Real</u> God
   Of all-and-All),
here Appearing
As The Ruchira Avatar,
The Avataric Incarnation Of The "Bright" Divine
   Love-Bliss,
Adi Da Samraj—
Who <u>Is</u> The First Person,
The Eternal and Ever-Free Avadhoota,[9]
The One and Only Heart
Of all-and-All
(Which <u>Is</u> The Non-Separate Divine Self
Of all-and-All),
and
Who <u>Is</u> The Divine Giver
(Of The "All" That <u>Is</u>)
To all-and-All,
and
Who <u>Is</u> The "All"-Gift Itself,
Which <u>Is</u> Eleutherios,
The Divine Liberator
(and The Divine Liberation)
Of all-and-All.

THE LIBERATOR (ELEUTHERIOS)

This Is The Heart-Liberating Word Of Eleutherios,
   The Divine Liberator,
   The Inherently egoless Acausal Personal Presence
   Of Reality and Truth
   (The all-and-All-Liberating
   Self-Condition and Source-Condition
   Of all-and-All,
   Which <u>Is</u> The Only and Acausal <u>Real</u> God
   Of all-and-All),
   here Appearing
   As The Ruchira Avatar,
   The Avataric Incarnation Of Infinite
      Love-Bliss-"Brightness" Itself,
   Adi Da Samraj—
   Who Is The Divine World-Teacher
   Promised For The "Late-Time",
   and
   Who Is The First, The Last, and The Only
   Divine Heart-Master,
   Whose Heart-Word
   Speaks
   To all conditionally Manifested beings,
   and
   Whose Divinely Self-"Emerging"[10]
   Heart-Blessing
   Spiritually Blesses
   all conditionally Manifested beings,
   and
   Whose Inherently Perfect Self-"Brightness"
   Divinely Liberates
   all conditionally Manifested beings—
   Freely,
   Liberally,
   Gracefully,
   and Without Ceasing—
   now, and forever hereafter.

NOTES TO THE TEXT OF
THE LIBERATOR (ELEUTHERIOS)

NOTES TO THE TEXT OF
THE LIBERATOR (ELEUTHERIOS)

Introduction to *The Liberator (Eleutherios)*

1. John 8:32.

2. The stories of many of Avatar Adi Da's Names and Titles can be found in *Adi Da: The Promised God-Man Is Here,* by Carolyn Lee.

3. Avatar Adi Da's devotees generally pronounce "Eleutherios" ELL-oo-THAIR-ee-ose.

4. Avatar Adi Da points out that, based on the surviving descriptions, it is not altogether clear what exactly occurred for Ramana Maharshi in this event. Avatar Adi Da notes that the existing accounts indicate the process of thought was still intact, and do not describe any Yogic evidence of a complete "death", although some spontaneous Samadhi of Transcendental Awareness might well have occurred.

5. Here Avatar Adi Da is referring to His Revelation of the esoteric visionary representation of Reality as a White Sphere in a black field—which Sphere is His own Divine Form.

The Liberator (Eleutherios)

6. When Avatar Adi Da communicates that He is "the First, the Last, and the Only Divine Heart-Master", He is not making exclusive claims that Enlightenment is not possible for (apparent) others. Rather, He is describing His Very Divine Person and the unique Avataric Divine nature of His human Birth and Life-Demonstration. Once the seventh stage Way of Adidam has been Revealed in the cosmic domain, via His Avataric Divine Demonstration, it is not necessary for another to do so. However, any of Avatar Adi Da's devotees who Realize the seventh stage Awakening will Awaken to and as His Perfect Divine Self-Condition, beyond all ego-presumptions of separateness and "difference".

7. This is a reference to the Artwork Created by Avatar Adi Da Samraj—specifically, His Artwork Created since 1999, in the Making of which Avatar Adi Da has Worked with the camera as a technical means, using photographic images as "blueprints" for the fabrication of monumental artforms.

8. Avatar Adi Da Samraj has Revealed that He Exists simultaneously in three Avataric Divine Forms—physical (His bodily human Form), Spiritual (His Spiritual Presence), and the Formlessness of Self-Existing and

THE LIBERATOR (ELEUTHERIOS)

Self-Radiant Consciousness Itself (His Very State). The fundamental practice of heart-Communion with Him includes heart-Communion with all three aspects of His Being—always (from the very beginning of the practice of the Way of Adidam through the seventh stage of life) founded in devotional recognition-response to His Avatarically-Born bodily (human) Divine Form and Person.

9. Avadhoot is a traditional term for one who has "shaken off" or "passed beyond" all worldly attachments and cares, including all motives of detachment (or conventional and other-worldly renunciation), all conventional notions of life and religion, and all seeking for "answers" or "solutions" in the form of conditional experience or conditional knowledge. Therefore, in reference to Avatar Adi Da Samraj, the Title "Avadhoota" indicates the Inherently Perfect Freedom of the One Who knows His Identity as the Acausal Divine Person and Who thus "Always Already" Stands Free of the binding and deluding power of conditional existence.

10. On January 11, 1986, Avatar Adi Da passed through a profound Yogic Swoon, Which He later described as the Yogic Establishment of His Avataric Divine Self-"Emergence". Avatar Adi Da's Avataric Divine Self-"Emergence" is an ongoing Process in which His Avatarically-Born bodily (human) Divine Form has been (and is ever more profoundly and potently being) conformed to Himself, the Very Divine Person, such that His bodily (human) Form is now (and forever hereafter) an utterly Unobstructed Sign and Agent of His own Divine Being. For Avatar Adi Da's extended description of His Avataric Divine Self-"Emergence", see Part Three of *The Knee Of Listening*.

GLOSSARY

GLOSSARY

Adi—Sanskrit for "first", "primordial", "source"—also "primary", "beginning". Thus, the Divine Name "Adi Da" expresses the Truth that Avatar Adi Da is the Primordial Being, the Source of all, the Original Divine Person.

Adidam—When Avatar Adi Da Samraj first Gave the name "Adidam" (in January 1996) to the Way He has Revealed, He pointed out that the final "m" adds a mantric force, evoking the effect of the primal Sanskrit syllable "Om". (For Avatar Adi Da's Revelation of the most profound esoteric significance of "Om" as the Divine Sound of His own Very Being, see *The Dawn Horse Testament*.) Simultaneously, the final "m" suggests the English word "Am" (expressing "I Am"), such that the Name "Adidam" also evokes Avatar Adi Da's Primal Self-Confession, "I Am Adi Da", or, more simply, "I Am Da" (or, in Sanskrit, "Aham Da Asmi").

all-and-All—A phrase Avatar Adi Da has created to describe the totality of conditional existence—both as the "sum of its parts" and as an undivided whole. He defines lower-case "all" as indicating "the collected sum of all Presumed To Be Separate (or limited) beings, things, and conditions", and upper-case "All" as indicating "The All (or The Undivided Totality) Of conditional Existence As A Whole".

Avataric Incarnation—The Divinely Descended Embodiment of the Divine Person. The reference "Avataric Incarnation" indicates that Avatar Adi Da Samraj fulfills both the traditional expectation of the East, that the True God-Man is an Avatar (or an utterly Divine "Descent" of Real Acausal God in conditionally manifested form), and the traditional expectation of the West, that the True God-Man is an Incarnation (or an utterly human Embodiment of Real Acausal God).

"Bright"—By the word "Bright" (and its variations, such as "Brightness"), Avatar Adi Da refers to the Self-Existing and Self-Radiant Divine Reality that He has Revealed since His Birth. Avatar Adi Da Named His own Self-Evidently Divine Self-Condition "the 'Bright'" in His Infancy, as soon as He acquired the capability of language.

This term is placed in quotation marks to indicate that Avatar Adi Da uses it with the specific meaning described here.

the Circle—The Circle of the body-mind is a primary pathway of natural life-energy and the Divine Spirit-Energy in the body-mind. It is composed of two arcs: the descending Current, which flows through the frontal line—down the front of the body, from the crown of the head to the bodily base—and which corresponds to the gross dimension of the body-mind; and the ascending Current, which flows through the

THE LIBERATOR (ELEUTHERIOS)

spinal line—up the back of the body, from the bodily base to the crown of the head—and which corresponds to the subtle dimension of the body-mind.

"consideration"—Avatar Adi Da uses this word to refer to "a process of one-pointed (but, ultimately, thoughtless) concentration and exhaustive contemplation of a particular object, function, person, process, or condition, until the essence or ultimate obviousness of that object is clear" [*Love of the Two-Armed Form*]. (Such a process was originally described by Patanjali, in his *Yoga Sutras*, as "samyama".)

This term is placed in quotation marks to indicate that Avatar Adi Da uses it with the specific technical meaning described here.

As engaged in the Way of Adidam, "consideration" is not merely an intellectual investigation. It is the participatory investment of one's whole being. If one "considers" something fully—in the context of one's practice of devotion to Avatar Adi Da and study of His Wisdom-Teaching—this concentration results "in both the deepest intuition and the most practical grasp of the Lawful and Divine necessities of human existence" [*Love of the Two-Armed Form*].

Cosmic Mandala—The Sanskrit word "mandala" (literally, "circle") is commonly used in the esoteric Spiritual traditions of the East to describe the hierarchical levels of cosmic existence. "Mandala" also denotes an artistic rendering of a visionary representation of the cosmos. Avatar Adi Da uses the phrase "Cosmic Mandala" as a reference to the totality of the conditionally manifested cosmos (or all worlds, forms, and beings), which (He has Revealed) can be visually perceived (and, thus, represented) as a pattern of concentric circular bands (or, more accurately, spheres) of certain distinct colors (each of a particular relative width), with a Brilliant White Five-Pointed Star at the center.

Da—Avatar Adi Da's Divine Name "Da" means "The One Who Gives", or "The Divine Giver". This Name was spontaneously Revealed to Avatar Adi Da as His Principal Divine Name—and it is a syllable with great sacred significance in various cultures. Tibetan Buddhists regard the syllable "Da" (written, in Tibetan, with a single symbol) as most auspicious, and they assign numerous sacred meanings to it, including "Entrance into the Dharma". In the most ancient of the Upanishads (the *Brihadaranyaka Upanishad*), the Divine Being gives the fundamental instruction necessary for each of the different classes of living beings by uttering the single sound "Da". (Each class of beings understands "Da" in the manner uniquely necessary in their case.) In this passage, "Da" is said to be the Divine Voice that can be heard speaking through thunder (S. Radhakrishnan, trans., *The Principal Upanishads* [Atlantic Highlands, N.J.: Humanities Press International, 1st paperback ed., 1992], 289–90).

Glossary

Da Avatar—The Divine Descent (Avatar) of the One and True Divine Giver (Da).

"difference"—The root of the egoic presumption of separateness—in contrast with the Realization of Oneness, or Non-"Difference", Which is Native to the Self-Existing Divine Self-Condition. This term is placed in quotation marks to indicate that Avatar Adi Da uses it in the "so to speak" sense. He is Communicating (by means of the quotation marks) that, in Reality, there is no such thing as "difference", even though it appears to be the case from the "point of view" of ordinary human perception.

Divine "Bright" Self-Domain—Avatar Adi Da affirms that there is a Divine Self-Domain that is the Perfectly Subjective Condition of the conditional worlds. It is not "elsewhere", not an objective "place" (like a subtle "heaven" or mythical "paradise"), but It is the Self-Evidently Divine Source-Condition of every conditionally manifested being and thing—and It is not other than Avatar Adi Da Himself. Avatar Adi Da Reveals that His Divine Self-Domain is a Boundless (and Boundlessly "Bright") Sphere. To Realize the seventh stage of life (by the Divine Spiritual Grace of Avatar Adi Da Samraj) is to Awaken to His Divine Self-Domain. See *The Dawn Horse Testament*.

Divine Transfiguration—See **four phases of the seventh stage of life**.

Divine Transformation—See **four phases of the seventh stage of life**.

Divine Translation—See **four phases of the seventh stage of life**.

Divine World-Teacher—Avatar Adi Da Samraj is the Divine World-Teacher because His Wisdom-Teaching is the uniquely Perfect Instruction to every being—in this (and every) world—relative to the total process of Divine Enlightenment. Furthermore, Avatar Adi Da Samraj constantly Extends His Regard to the entire world (and the entire cosmic domain)—not on the political or social level, but as a Spiritual matter, constantly Working to Bless and Purify all beings everywhere.

ego-"I"—The fundamental activity of self-contraction, or the presumption of separate and separative existence.

The "I" is placed in quotation marks to indicate that it is used by Avatar Adi Da in the "so to speak" sense. He is Communicating (by means of the quotation marks) that, in Reality, there is no such thing as the separate "I", even though it appears to be the case from the "point of view" of ordinary human perception.

feeling of relatedness—In the foundation stages of practice in the Way of Adidam, the basic (or gross) manifestation of the avoidance of relationship is understood and released when Avatar Adi Da's devotee hears Him (or comes to the point of most fundamental self-understanding), thereby regaining the free capability for simple relatedness, or living on the basis of the feeling of relatedness rather than the avoidance of relationship. Nevertheless, the feeling of relatedness is not Ultimate Realization, because it is still founded in the presumption of a "difference" between "I" and "other". Only in the "Perfect Practice" of Adidam is the feeling of relatedness itself fully understood as the root-act of attention and, ultimately, transcended in the Tacit Self-Apprehension of Being.

four phases of the seventh stage of life—Avatar Adi Da has Revealed that the Awakening to the seventh stage of life is not an "endpoint" but is (rather) the beginning of the final Spiritual process. One of the unique aspects of Avatar Adi Da's Revelation is His precise description of the seventh stage process as consisting of four phases: Divine Transfiguration, Divine Transformation, Divine Indifference, and Divine Translation.

The First Sign (or Demonstration) Of The Only-By-Me Revealed and Given Seventh Stage Of Life (In The "Radical" Way Of The Heart) Is Divine Transfiguration, *In Which the body-mind Of My By-My-Avataric-Divine-Spiritual-Grace-Enlightened Devotee Is Self-Radiant With My Avatarically Self-Transmitted Divine Love-Bliss, Spontaneously Blessing all of the (Apparent) relations of the body-mind.*

The Second Sign (or Demonstration) Of The Only-By-Me Revealed and Given Seventh Stage Of Life (In The "Radical" Way Of The Heart) Is Divine Transformation, *In Which the body-mind Of My By-My-Avataric-Divine-Spiritual-Grace-Enlightened Devotee Effectively Exhibits The Only-By-Me Revealed and Given Signs and Powers Of Real (Acausal) God.*

The Third Sign (or Demonstration) Of The Only-By-Me Revealed and Given Seventh Stage Of Life (In The "Radical" Way Of The Heart) Is Divine Indifference, *In Which Even the body-mind Of My By-My-Avataric-Divine-Spiritual-Grace-Enlightened Devotee Is Pre-Occupied With The Self-Existing Event Of My Self-Radiant Love-Bliss, and the world of (Apparent) relations Is (More and More) Minimally and Not Otherwise Noticed. . . .*

The Final Sign (or Demonstration) Of The Only-By-Me Revealed and Given Seventh Stage Of Life (and Of The Total Practice Of The Only-By-Me Revealed and Given "Radical" Way Of The Heart) Is The Great Event Of Divine Translation—*Which Is . . . The Process Of Transition To (or "Dawning"* As*) My Divine Self-Domain Via The Divinely "Bright" Outshining Of The Cosmic Domain In The Only-By-Me Revealed and Given Divine Sphere and Sign Of The "Midnight Sun" (Most Perfectly Beyond and Prior To all-and-All Of Cosmic, or conditional, forms, beings, signs, conditions, relations, and things).*

—Avatar Adi Da Samraj
The Dawn Horse Testament

Glossary

frontal Yoga—The process whereby knots and obstructions in the frontal personality are penetrated, opened, surrendered, and released, through the devotee's reception of Avatar Adi Da's Spiritual Transmission in the frontal line of the body-mind. "Frontal Yoga" is synonymous with the process of listening, hearing, and seeing, leading up to the "Perfect Practice" (see **listening, hearing, seeing** and **"Perfect Practice"**).

hearing—See **listening, hearing, seeing**.

Inherent (or Tacit) Self-Apprehension of Being—The uncaused, unqualified, direct, and wordless intuition of the Self-Evidently Divine Self-Condition.

Kundalini Yoga—A tradition of Yogic techniques in which practice is devoted to awakening the internal energy processes, which bring about subtle experiences and blisses. But, as Avatar Adi Da has indicated, the true manifestation of Spiritual Awakening is spontaneous, a Grace Given in the Company of a True Siddha-Guru, and in the midst of an entire life of practice in his or her Company.

"late-time" (or "dark" epoch)—Avatar Adi Da uses the terms "late-time" and "'dark' epoch" to describe the present era—in which doubt of God (and of anything at all beyond mortal existence) is more and more pervading the entire world, and the self-interest of the separate individual is more and more regarded to be the ultimate principle of life.

These terms include quotation marks to indicate that they are used by Avatar Adi Da in the "so to speak" sense. In this case, He is Communicating (by means of the quotation marks) that, in Reality, the "darkness" of this apparent "late-time" is not Reality, or Truth, but only an appearance from the "point of view" of ordinary human perception.

listening, hearing, seeing—Avatar Adi Da describes the entire course of the Way of Adidam as falling into four primary phases:

1. listening to Him
2. hearing Him
3. seeing Him
4. the "Perfect Practice" of Identifying with Him

For a description of the unfolding phases of practice of Adidam, see *Adidam: The True World-Religion Given by the Promised God-Man, Adi Da Samraj* and *The Dawn Horse Testament*.

"Listening" is Avatar Adi Da's technical term for the beginning practice of the Way of Adidam. A listening devotee literally "listens" to Avatar Adi Da's Instruction and applies it in his or her life.

The core of the listening process (and of all future practice of the Way of Adidam) is the practice of Ruchira Avatara Bhakti Yoga (or turning the four principal faculties of the body-mind—body, emotion, mind, and breath—to Him)—conjoined with the preliminary practice of "Perfect Knowledge"—and supported by practice of the "conscious process" and "conductivity", and by the embrace of the functional, practical, relational, and cultural disciplines Given by Him. It is during the listening phase (once the foundation practice is fully established) that the devotee applies to come on extended formal retreat in Avatar Adi Da's physical Company (or, after His physical Lifetime, in the physical company, and the by-Him-Spiritually-Empowered circumstances, of the Ruchira Sannyasin Order of Adidam Ruchiradam). In the retreat circumstance, when the rightly prepared devotee truly (whole bodily) turns the principal faculties to Him, Avatar Adi Da is spontaneously Moved to Grant His Spiritual Initiation (or Ruchira Shaktipat), such that the devotee can become more and more consistently capable of tangibly receiving His Spiritual Transmission. This is the beginning of the Spiritually Awakened practice of the Way of Adidam—when the devotional relationship to Avatar Adi Da becomes (by His Divine Spiritual Grace) the devotional-and-Spiritual relationship to Him. The phase of listening to Avatar Adi Da, rightly and effectively engaged, eventually culminates (by His Divine Spiritual Grace) in the true hearing of Him. The devotee has begun to hear Avatar Adi Da when there is most fundamental understanding of the root-act of egoity (or self-contraction), or the unique capability to consistently transcend the self-contraction. The capability of true hearing is not something the ego can "achieve". That capability can only be Granted, by Means of Avatar Adi Da's Divine Spiritual Grace, to His devotee who has effectively completed the (eventually, Spiritually Awakened) process of listening.

When Spiritually Awakened practice of the Way of Adidam is magnified by means of the hearing-capability, the devotee has the necessary preparation to (in due course) engage that Spiritually Awakened practice in the fully technically responsible manner. This is another point (in the course of the Way of Adidam) when the devotee engages an extended formal retreat in Avatar Adi Da's physical Company (or, after His physical Lifetime, in the physical company, and the by-Him-Spiritually-Empowered circumstances, of the Ruchira Sannyasin Order of Adidam Ruchiradam). In this case, in Response to the devotee's more mature practice of devotional and Spiritual resort to Him, Avatar Adi Da Gives the Initiatory Spiritual Gift of Upward-turned Spiritual receptivity of Him (as He describes in His "Source-Text" *Hridaya Rosary*). This is Avatar Adi Da's Spiritual Initiation of His devotee into the seeing phase of practice, which Avatar Adi Da describes as the "fully technically responsible" form of Spiritually Awakened Communion with Him.

One of the principal signs of the transition from the listening-hearing practice to the both-hearing-and-seeing practice is emotional conversion from the reactive emotions that characterize egoic

Glossary

self-obsession, to the openhearted, Radiant Happiness that characterizes fully technically responsible Spiritual devotion to Avatar Adi Da. This true and stable emotional conversion coincides with stable Upward-to-Him-turned receptivity of Avatar Adi Da's Spiritual Transmission.

As the process of seeing develops, the body-mind becomes more and more fully Infused by Avatar Adi Da's Spirit-Baptism, purified of any psycho-physical patterning that <u>diminishes</u> that reception. With increasing maturity in the seeing process, Avatar Adi Da's Transmission of the "Bright" is experienced in the unique form that He describes as "the 'Thumbs'"—and, through this process, the devotee is gracefully grown entirely beyond identification with the body-mind. The seeing process is complete when the devotee receives Avatar Adi Da's Gift of Spiritually Awakening as the Witness-Consciousness (That Stands Prior to body, mind, and world, and even the act of attention itself). This Awakening to the Witness-Consciousness marks readiness for another period of Initiatory retreat in Avatar Adi Da's physical Company (or, after His physical Lifetime, in the physical company, and the by-Him-Spiritually-Empowered circumstances, of the Ruchira Sannyasin Order of Adidam Ruchiradam), in which He Spiritually Initiates the devotee into the "Perfect Practice".

"Locate"—To "Locate" Avatar Adi Da is to "Truly Heart-Find"

Him. Avatar Adi Da places this term (and its variants) in quotation marks to indicate the sense of "so to speak"—because He is, in reality, Omnipresent, without any specific "location".

Love-Ananda Avatar—The Very Incarnation of the Divine Love-Bliss.

"misses the mark"—"Hamartia" (the word in New Testament Greek that was translated into English as "sin") was also an archery term meaning "missing the mark".

Most Perfect / Most Ultimate—Avatar Adi Da uses the phrase "Most Perfect(ly)" in the sense of "Absolutely Perfect(ly)". Similarly, the phrase "Most Ultimate(ly)" is equivalent to "Absolutely Ultimate(ly)". "Most Perfect(ly)" and "Most Ultimate(ly)" are always references to the seventh (or Divinely Enlightened) stage of life. "Perfect(ly)" and "Ultimate(ly)" (without "Most") refer to the practice and Realization in the context of the "Perfect Practice" of the Way of Adidam (or, when Avatar Adi Da is making reference to the Great Tradition, to practice and Realization in the context of the sixth stage of life).

"Narcissus"—In Avatar Adi Da's Teaching-Revelation, "Narcissus" is a key symbol of the un-Enlightened individual as a self-obsessed seeker, enamored of his or her own self-image and egoic self-consciousness.

THE LIBERATOR (ELEUTHERIOS)

He is the ancient one visible in the Greek myth, who was the universally adored child of the gods, who rejected the loved-one and every form of love and relationship, and who was finally condemned to the contemplation of his own image—until, as a result of his own act and obstinacy, he suffered the fate of eternal separateness and died in infinite solitude.

—Avatar Adi Da Samraj
The Knee Of Listening

When Avatar Adi Da uses "Narcissus" as an archetypal reference to the activity of self-contraction, He places the name in quotation marks, to indicate that He is using the name metaphorically (rather than in reference to the character in the Greek myth). When He uses "Narcissus" in reference to the mythological character, the name is not placed in quotation marks. Avatar Adi Da uses the adjective "Narcissistic" in the sense of "relating to the activity of self-contraction", rather than in any more conventional meaning (particularly those meanings associated with the discipline of psychology).

"Open Eyes"—"Open Eyes" is Avatar Adi Da's technical synonym for the Realization of the seventh stage of life, or Most Perfect Divine Enlightenment. The phrase graphically describes the non-exclusive, non-inward, Prior State of the Divine Self-Realizer, Who is Identified Non-conditionally with the Divine Self-Reality, while also allowing whatever arises to appear in the Divine Consciousness.

This term is placed in quotation marks to indicate that Avatar Adi Da uses it with the specific technical meaning described here (rather than any of the more commonly accepted general meanings).

Outshine—"Outshine" and its variants refer to the process of Divine Translation, the final Demonstration of the four-phase process of the seventh stage of life in the Way of Adidam. In the Great Event of Outshining (or Divine Translation), body, mind, and world are no longer noticed—not because one has withdrawn or dissociated from conditionally manifested phenomena, but because the Self-Abiding Divine Self-Recognition of all arising phenomena as modifications of the Divine Acausal Self-Condition has become so intense that the "Bright" Divine Conscious Light now Outshines all such phenomena.

"Perfect Contemplation"—A technical term Avatar Adi Da uses to describe formal occasions of Communion with Him when the practitioner has been established in the "Perfect Practice" of Adidam. "Perfect Contemplation" is no longer any kind of exercise of the faculties of the body-mind (as is "meditation"), but rather is established as effortless "Contemplation" of Avatar Adi Da as Consciousness Itself, Prior to body and mind.

"Perfect Practice"—The "Perfect Practice" is Avatar Adi Da's technical term for the discipline of the most

Glossary

mature stages of practice in the Way of Adidam. The "Perfect Practice" is practice in the Domain of Consciousness Itself (as opposed to practice from the "point of view" of the body or the mind). The "Perfect Practice" unfolds in three phases, the third of which is Divine Enlightenment. This term is placed in quotation marks to indicate that Avatar Adi Da uses it with the specific technical meaning described here.

Perfectly Subjective—Avatar Adi Da uses this phrase to describe the True Divine Source (or "Subject") of the conditionally manifested worlds—as opposed to regarding the Acausal Divine as some sort of objective "Other". Thus, in the phrase "Perfectly Subjective", the word "Subjective" does not have the sense of "relating to the inward experience of an individual", but, rather, it has the sense of "Being Consciousness Itself, the True 'Subject' of all apparent experience".

"Point of View" / "point of view"—In Avatar Adi Da's Wisdom-Teaching, "Point of View" is capitalized when referring to the "Position" of Consciousness Itself, Prior to (and independent of) the body-mind or conditional existence altogether. The "Point of View" of Consciousness Itself is the basis of the "Perfect Practice" of the Way of Adidam. Both terms are in quotation marks to indicate that Avatar Adi Da uses them in the "so to speak" sense. He is Communicating (by means of the quotation marks) that, in Reality, there is no such thing as a "point of view", even though it appears to be the case from the "point of view" of ordinary human perception.

"radical"—Derived from the Latin "radix", meaning "root". Thus, "radical" principally means "irreducible", "fundamental", or "relating to the origin". Thus, Avatar Adi Da defines "radical" as "at-the-root". Because Avatar Adi Da uses "radical" in this literal sense, it appears in quotation marks in His Wisdom-Teaching, in order to distinguish His usage from the common reference to an extreme (often political) view.

"Radical" Way of the Heart—The Way Avatar Adi Da Offers is the "Radical" Way of the Heart Itself, Which Is Real (Acausal) God, the Divine Self-Condition, the Divine Reality. He calls the Way of the Heart He has Revealed and Given "Radical", because it is always already "at-the-root", or Inherently Established in the Prior Condition of Reality Itself.

Ramana Maharshi—Ramana Maharshi (1879–1950) is regarded by many as the greatest Indian Sage of the twentieth century. Following a spontaneous death-like event as a teenager, he abandoned home for a life of Spiritual practice. Eventually, an ashram, which still exists today, was established around him at Tiruvannamalai in South India.

right side of the heart—See **stations of the heart**.

THE LIBERATOR (ELEUTHERIOS)

Ruchira Avatar—In Sanskrit, "Ruchira" means "bright, radiant, effulgent". Thus, the Reference "Ruchira Avatar" indicates that Avatar Adi Da Samraj is the "Bright" (or Radiant) Descent of the Divine Reality Itself into the conditionally manifested worlds, Appearing here in His bodily (human) Divine Form.

Rudi—Swami Rudrananda (1928–1973), or Albert Rudolph (known as "Rudi"), was Avatar Adi Da's first human Teacher—from 1964 to 1968, in New York City. Rudi served Avatar Adi Da Samraj in the development of basic practical life-disciplines and the frontal Yoga, which is the process whereby knots and obstructions in the physical and etheric dimensions of the body-mind are penetrated, opened, surrendered, and released through Spiritual reception in the frontal line of the body-mind. Rudi's own Teachers included Swami Muktananda (with whom Rudi studied for many years) and Bhagavan Nityananda (the Indian Adept-Realizer who was also Swami Muktananda's Guru). Rudi met Bhagavan Nityananda shortly before Bhagavan Nityananda's death, and Rudi always thereafter acknowledged Bhagavan Nityananda as his original and principal Guru.

sadhana—In Sanskrit, "sadhana" means "ego-transcending religious or Spiritual practice".

Samadhi—The Sanskrit word "Samadhi" traditionally denotes various exalted states that appear in the context of esoteric meditation and Realization. Avatar Adi Da Teaches that, for His devotees, Samadhi is, even more simply and fundamentally, the Enjoyment of His Divine State (or "Divine Samadhi"), Which is experienced (even from the beginning of the practice of Adidam) through ego-transcending heart-Communion with Him. Therefore, "the cultivation of Samadhi" is another way to describe the fundamental basis of the Way of Adidam. Avatar Adi Da's devotee is in Samadhi in any moment of standing beyond the separate self in true devotional heart-Communion with Him. See *The Dawn Horse Testament*.

seeing—See **listening, hearing, and seeing**.

Self-Abiding Divine Self-Recognition—Self-Abiding Divine Self-Recognition is the ego-transcending and world-transcending Intelligence of the Divine Self-Condition in relation to all conditional phenomena. The devotee of Avatar Adi Da who Realizes the seventh stage of life simply Self-Abides As the Divine Conscious Light Itself, and he or she Freely Self-Recognizes (or inherently and instantly and most perfectly comprehends and perceives) all phenomena (including body, mind, conditional self, and conditional world) as transparent (or merely apparent), and unnecessary, and inherently non-binding modifications of the same "Bright" Conscious Light.

Glossary

self-contraction—The fundamental presumption (and activity) of separation.

Self-Existing and Self-Radiant—"Self-Existing" and "Self-Radiant" are terms describing the two fundamental aspects of the One Divine Person (or Reality)—Existence (or Being, or Consciousness) Itself, and Radiance (or Energy, or Light) Itself.

Self-Recognition. See **Self-Abiding Divine Self-Recognition**.

seventh stage of life. See **stages of life**.

Siddhi—Sanskrit for "power", or "accomplishment". When capitalized in Avatar Adi Da's Wisdom-Teaching, "Siddhi" is the Spiritual, Transcendental, and Divine Awakening-Power That He spontaneously and effortlessly Transmits to all.

stages of life—Avatar Adi Da Samraj describes the potential experiences and Realizations of humankind in terms of seven stages of life. This schema is one of Avatar Adi Da's unique Gifts to humanity—His precise "mapping" of the potential developmental course of human experience as it unfolds through the gross, subtle, and causal dimensions of the being. He describes this course in terms of six stages of life—which account for, and correspond to, all possible orientations to Reality (both conditional and Non-conditional) that have arisen in human history. His own Avataric Divine Self-Revelation—the Realization of the "Bright", Prior to all experience—is the seventh stage of life. Understanding this structure of seven stages illuminates the unique nature of Avatar Adi Da's "Sadhana Years" (and of the Spiritual process in His Company). See book one of the "Perfect Knowledge" Series for a full description.

stations of the heart—Avatar Adi Da distinguishes three stations of the heart, associated (respectively) with the right side, the middle station (traditionally called the "anahata chakra"), and the left side of the heart region of the chest. He Reveals that these stations are the loci (or focal points of living origination) of the causal body, the subtle body, and the gross body (respectively). Avatar Adi Da Teaches (as foreshadowed in certain rare sixth stage texts) that the primal psycho-physical seat of Consciousness and of attention is associated with what He calls the "right side of the heart". He has Revealed that this center (which is neither the heart chakra nor the gross physical heart) corresponds to the sinoatrial node (or "pacemaker"), the source of the gross physical heartbeat in the right atrium (or upper right chamber) of the physical heart. In the Event of Divine Self-Realization, there is a unique process in which the ego-knot in the right side of the heart is released—and it is because of this connection between the

THE LIBERATOR (ELEUTHERIOS)

right side of the heart and Divine Self-Realization that Avatar Adi Da uses the term "the True Heart" as another form of reference to the Divine Acausal Self-Condition.

Swami Muktananda—The second Teacher in Avatar Adi Da's Lineage of Blessing was Swami Muktananda (1908–1982), who was born in Mangalore, South India. Having left home at the age of fifteen, he wandered for many years, seeking the Divine Truth from sources all over India. Eventually, he came under the Spiritual Influence of Bhagavan Nityananda, whom he recognized as his Guru and in whose Spiritual Company he mastered Kundalini Yoga. Swami Muktananda served Avatar Adi Da as Guru during the period from 1968 to 1970. In the summer of 1969, during Avatar Adi Da's second visit to India, Swami Muktananda wrote a letter confirming Avatar Adi Da's attainment of "Yogic Liberation", and acknowledging His right to Teach others. However, from the beginning of their relationship, Swami Muktananda instructed Avatar Adi Da to visit Bhagavan Nityananda's burial site every day (whenever Avatar Adi Da was at Swami Muktananda's Ashram in Ganeshpuri, India) as a means to surrender to Bhagavan Nityananda as the Supreme Guru of the Lineage.

Witness / Witness-Consciousness / Witness-Position—When Consciousness is Free of identification with the body-mind, It Stands in Its natural "Position" as the Conscious Witness of all that arises to and in and as the body-mind.

In the Way of Adidam, the stable Realization of the Witness-Position is a Spiritual Gift from Avatar Adi Da, made possible by (and necessarily following upon) the reception of His Spiritual Gift of the "Thumbs". The stable Realization of the Witness-Position is the characteristic of the first stage of the "Perfect Practice". See *The Dawn Horse Testament*.

The Avataric Great Sage,
ADI DA SAMRAJ

AN INVITATION
Become a Formal Devotee of Avatar Adi Da Samraj

In the depth of every human being, there is a profound need for answers to the fundamental questions of existence. Is there a God? What is beyond this life? Why is there suffering? What is Truth? What is Reality?

In this book, you have been introduced to the Wisdom-Revelation of Avatar Adi Da, whose Teachings truly and completely address all of these fundamental questions. How can Avatar Adi Da resolve these fundamental questions? Because He speaks, not from the "point of view" of the human dilemma, but directly from the unique Freedom of His Divine State. Adi Da's Birth in 1939 was an intentional embrace of the human situation, for the sake of Revealing the Way of Divine Liberation to all and Offering the Spiritual Blessing that carries beings to that true Freedom. He is thus the fulfillment of the ancient intuitions of the "Avatar"—the One Who Appears in human Form, as a direct manifestation of the Unmanifest Reality.

Through a 28-year process of Teaching-Work (beginning in 1972), Avatar Adi Da established the Way of Adidam—the Way of the devotional and Spiritual relationship to Him. In those years of Teaching, He spoke for many hours with groups of His devotees—always looking for them, as representatives of humanity, to ask all of their questions about God, Truth, Reality, and human life. In response, He Gave the ecstatic Way of heart-Communion with Him, and all the details of how that process unfolds. Thus, He created a new tradition, based on His direct Revelation (as Avatar) of the Divine Reality.

THE LIBERATOR (ELEUTHERIOS)

Avatar Adi Da Samraj does not offer you a set of beliefs, or even a set of Spiritual techniques. He simply Offers you His Revelation of Truth as a Free Gift. If you are moved to take up His Way, He invites you to enter into an extraordinarily deep and transformative devotional and Spiritual relationship to Him. On the following pages, we present a number of ways that you can choose to deepen your response to Adi Da Samraj and consider becoming His formal devotee.

To find Avatar Adi Da Samraj is to find the Very Heart of Reality—tangibly felt in your own heart as the Deepest Truth of Existence. This is the great mystery that you are invited to discover. ■

Adidam is not a conventional religion.
Adidam is not a conventional way of life.
Adidam is about the transcending of the ego-"I".
Adidam is about the Freedom of Divine Self-Realization.

Adidam is not based on mythology or belief.
Adidam is a "reality practice".
Adidam is a "reality consideration", in which the various modes of egoity are progressively transcended.

Adidam is a universally applicable Way of life.
Adidam is for those who will choose It, and whose hearts and intelligence fully respond to Me and My Offering.
Adidam is a Great Revelation, and It is to be freely and openly communicated to all.

AVATAR ADI DA SAMRAJ

For what you can do next to respond to Avatar Adi Da's Offering, or to simply find out more about Him and the Way of Adidam, please use the information given in the following pages.

**Contact an Adidam center near you
for courses and events**
(p. 144)

Visit our website: www.adidam.org
(p. 145)

**For young people:
Join the Adidam Youth Fellowship**
(p. 146)

**Support Avatar Adi Da's Work
and the Way of Adidam**
(p. 146)

**Order other books and recordings
by and about Avatar Adi Da Samraj**
(pp. 147–51)

Contact an Adidam center near you

■ To find out about becoming a formal devotee of Avatar Adi Da, and for information about upcoming courses, events, and seminars in your area:

AMERICAS
12040 North Seigler Road
Middletown, CA 95461 USA
1-707-928-4936

PACIFIC-ASIA
12 Seibel Road
Henderson
Auckland 1008
New Zealand
64-9-838-9114

AUSTRALIA
P.O. Box 244
Kew 3101
Victoria
**1800 ADIDAM
(1800-234-326)**

EUROPE-AFRICA
Annendaalderweg 10
6105 AT Maria Hoop
The Netherlands
31 (0)20 468 1442

THE UNITED KINGDOM
uk@adidam.org
0845-330-1008

INDIA
Shree Love-Ananda Marg
Rampath, Shyam Nagar Extn.
Jaipur–302 019, India
91 (141) 2293080

E-MAIL:
correspondence@adidam.org

■ For more contact information about local Adidam groups, please see **www.adidam.org/centers**

**Visit our website:
www.adidam.org**

- **SEE AUDIO-VISUAL PRESENTATIONS** on the Divine Life and Spiritual Revelation of Avatar Adi Da Samraj

- **LISTEN TO DISCOURSES** Given by Avatar Adi Da Samraj to His practicing devotees—
  - Transcending egoic notions of God
  - Why Reality cannot be grasped by the mind
  - How the devotional relationship to Avatar Adi Da moves you beyond ego-bondage
  - The supreme process of Spiritual Transmission

- **READ QUOTATIONS** from the "Source-Texts" of Avatar Adi Da Samraj—
  - Real God as the only Reality
  - The ancient practice of Guru-devotion
  - The two opposing life-strategies characteristic of the West and the East—and the way beyond both
  - The Prior Unity at the root of all that exists
  - The limits of scientific materialism
  - The true religion beyond all seeking
  - The esoteric structure of the human being
  - The real process of death and reincarnation
  - The nature of Divine Enlightenment

- **SUBSCRIBE** to the online *Adidam Revelation* magazine

For young people:
Join the Adidam Youth Fellowship

■ Young people under 21 can participate in the "Adidam Youth Fellowship"—either as a "friend" or practicing member. Adidam Youth Fellowship members participate in study programs, retreats, celebrations, and other events with other young people responding to Avatar Adi Da. To learn more about the Youth Fellowship, call or write:

Vision of Mulund Institute (VMI)
10336 Loch Lomond Road, PMB 146
Middletown, CA 95461
phone: (707) 928-6932
e-mail: vmi@adidam.org
www.visionofmulund.org

Support Avatar Adi Da's Work and the Way of Adidam

■ If you are moved to serve Avatar Adi Da's Spiritual Work specifically through advocacy and/or financial patronage, please contact:

Advocacy
12180 Ridge Road
Middletown, CA 95461
phone: (707) 928-5267
e-mail: adidam_advocacy@adidam.org

Order other books and recordings by and about Avatar Adi Da Samraj

ADI DA
The Promised God-Man Is Here

The biography of Avatar Adi Da from His Birth to present time. Includes a wealth of quotations from His Writings and Talks, as well as stories told by His devotees. 358 pp., **$16.95**

ADIDAM
The True World-Religion Given by the Promised God-Man, Adi Da Samraj

A direct and simple summary of the fundamental aspects of the Way of Adidam.
196 pp., **$16.95**

ADI DA AND ADIDAM
The Divine Self-Revelation of the Avataric Way of the "Bright" and the "Thumbs"

A brief introduction to Avatar Adi Da Samraj and His Unique Spiritual Revelation of the Way of Adidam. 64 pp., **$3.95**

THE LIBERATOR (ELEUTHERIOS)

THE KNEE OF LISTENING

The Divine Ordeal Of The Avataric Incarnation Of Conscious Light

The Spiritual Autobiography Of The Ruchira Avatar, Adi Da Samraj

Born in 1939 on Long Island, New York, Adi Da Samraj describes His earliest life as an existence of constant and unmitigated Spiritual "Brightness". His observation, still in infancy, that others did not live in this manner led Him to undertake an awesome quest—to discover why human beings suffer and how they can transcend that suffering. His quest led Him to a confrontation with the bleak despair of post-industrial Godlessness, to a minute examination of the workings of subjective awareness, to discipleship in a lineage of profound Yogis, to a period of intense Christian mysticism, and finally to a Re-Awakening to the perfect state of "Brightness" He had known at birth.

In *The Knee Of Listening,* Avatar Adi Da also reveals His own direct awareness of His "deeper-personality vehicles"—the beings whose lives were the direct antecedents (or the "pre-history") of His present human lifetime—the great nineteenth-century Indian Realizers Sri Ramakrishna and Swami Vivekananda. Finally, Avatar Adi Da describes the series of profound transformational events that took place in the decades after His Divine Re-Awakening—each one a form of "Yogic death" for which there is no recorded precedent.

Altogether, *The Knee Of Listening* is the unparalleled history of how the Divine Conscious Light has Incarnated in human form, in order to grant everyone the possibility of Ultimate Divine Liberation, Freedom, and Happiness.

The Knee Of Listening *is without a doubt the most profound Spiritual autobiography of all time.*

—**ROGER SAVOIE, PhD**
philosopher; translator; author, La Vipère et le Lion: La Voie radicale de la Spiritualité

822 pp., **$24.95**

MY "BRIGHT" WORD
by Adi Da Samraj

New Edition of the Classic Spiritual Discourses originally published as *The Method of the Siddhas*

In these Talks from the early years of His Teaching-Work, Avatar Adi Da Gives extraordinary Instruction on the foundation of True Spiritual life, covering topics such as the primary mechanism by which we are preventing the Realization of Truth, the means to overcome this mechanism, and the true function of the Spiritual Master in relation to the devotee.

In modern language, this volume teaches the ancient all-time trans-egoic truths. It transforms the student by paradox and by example. Consciousness, understanding, and finally the awakened Self are the rewards. What more can anyone want?

—**ELMER GREEN, PhD**
Director Emeritus, Center for Applied Psychophysiology,
The Menninger Clinic

544 pp., **$24.95**

BUDDHISM, ADVAITISM, AND THE WAY OF ADIDAM
a Talk by Avatar Adi Da Samraj

Rather than being about egoity and seeking, the Way of Adidam is about the magnification of the understanding of egoity and its seeking. It is about a Revealed Process that directly transcends egoity in every moment, rather than merely at the end.

—**AVATAR ADI DA SAMRAJ**
June 21, 1995

In this remarkable Talk, Avatar Adi Da gives a unique summary of the ultimate Realizations in Buddhism and Advaitism (or Advaita Vedanta), and describes the sympathetic likenesses between these traditions and the Way of Adidam. Avatar Adi Da clarifies the uniqueness of the Way of Adidam, which is not based on strategically excluding conditional reality, but on transcending it.

CD, 5 Tracks, total running time: 55 minutes
$16.95

THE LIBERATOR (ELEUTHERIOS)

LOVE AND BLESSINGS
The Divine Compassionate Miracles of Avatar Adi Da Samraj

In *Love and Blessings—The Divine Compassionate Miracles of Avatar Adi Da Samraj*, twenty-five of His devotees tell heart-breaking stories of human need and Divine Response. A soldier in Iraq, a woman going blind in Holland, a son with his dying father in Australia, a woman with cancer in America—these and others tell how they asked Adi Da Samraj for His Blessing-Regard and the miraculous process that ensued.

248 pp., **$19.95**

EASY DEATH
Spiritual Wisdom on the Ultimate Transcending of Death and Everything Else
by Adi Da Samraj

This new edition of *Easy Death* is thoroughly revised and updated with:

- New Talks and Essays from Avatar Adi Da on death and ultimate transcendence
- Accounts of profound Events of Yogic Death in Avatar Adi Da's own Life
- Stories of His Blessing in the death transitions of His devotees

. . . an exciting, stimulating, and thought-provoking book that adds immensely to the ever-increasing literature on the phenomena of life and death. But, more important, perhaps, it is a confirmation that a life filled with love instead of fear can lead to ultimately meaningful life and death.
   Thank you for this masterpiece.
                    —**ELISABETH KÜBLER-ROSS, MD**
                    author, *On Death and Dying*

544 pp., **$24.95**

Become a Formal Devotee of Avatar Adi Da Samraj

The Adidam Revelation Discourses on DVD

In July of 2004, Adi Da Samraj began a series of Discourses that were broadcast live over the internet to all His devotees around the world. During these remarkable occasions, Adi Da Samraj answered questions from those who were present in the room with Him, but also from devotees in other parts of the world via speakerphone. The "Adidam Revelation Discourse" DVDs offer you the opportunity to see and hear Avatar Adi Da speak in these unique and intimate occasions of Divine Instruction to His devotees. Current available titles include:

TRANSCEND THE SELF-KNOT OF FEAR
Running time: 60 minutes. Includes subtitles in English, Spanish, French, German, Dutch, and Polish.

THE DIVINE IS NOT THE CAUSE
Running time: 72 minutes. Includes subtitles in English, Spanish, French, German, Dutch, Finnish, Polish, Czech, Chinese, Japanese, and Hebrew.

CRACKING THE CODE OF EXPERIENCE
Running time: 86 minutes. Includes subtitles in English, Spanish, German, Dutch, Polish, Czech, Chinese, Japanese, and Hebrew.

DVD, **$26.95** each

To find out about and order other "Source-Texts", books, tapes, CDs, DVDs, and videos by and about Avatar Adi Da, contact your local Adidam regional center, or contact the Dawn Horse Press at:
1-877-770-0772 (from within North America)
1-707-928-6653 (from outside North America)
Or order online from: **www.dawnhorsepress.com**

The Five Books of the "Perfect Knowledge" Series

The books of the "Perfect Knowledge" Series are drawn from *Is: The "Perfect Knowledge" of Reality and The "Radical" Way to Realize It*, by the Avataric Great Sage, Adi Da Samraj.

The five books of the "Perfect Knowledge" Series together comprise the complete text of *Is*.

THE PERFECT TRADITION
*The Wisdom-Way of the Ancient Sages
and Its Fulfillment in the Way of "Perfect Knowledge"*
by The Avataric Great Sage, Adi Da Samraj

RELIGION AND REALITY
True Religion Is Not Belief in Any "God"-Idea but the Direct Experiential Realization of Reality Itself
by The Avataric Great Sage, Adi Da Samraj

THE LIBERATOR
*The "Radical" Reality-Teachings
of The Avataric Great Sage, Adi Da Samraj*

THE ANCIENT REALITY-TEACHINGS
*The Single Transcendental Truth Taught by
the Great Sages of Buddhism and Advaitism—
As Revealed by The Avataric Great Sage, Adi Da Samraj*

THE WAY OF PERFECT KNOWLEDGE
*The "Radical" Practice of Transcendental Spirituality
in the Way of Adidam*

by The Avataric Great Sage, Adi Da Samraj

The Avataric Divine Wisdom-Teaching of Adi Da Samraj

The Avataric Divine Wisdom-Teaching of Adi Da Samraj is gathered together, in its final form, in the many "Source-Texts" which He has designated as His Eternal Communication to humankind. These "Source-Texts" are "True-Water-Bearers", or Bearers of the "True Water" of the "Bright" Divine Reality Itself.

Avatar Adi Da has grouped His "Source-Texts" into twenty-three "Streams", or "Courses". Each of these Courses conveys a particular aspect of His Avataric Divine Wisdom-Teaching—and each Course (other than the first) may, in principle, include any number of "Source-Texts".

The first Course is Avatar Adi Da's paramount "Source-Text", *The Dawn Horse Testament Of The Ruchira Avatar*. The remaining twenty-two Courses are divided into two groups: *The Heart Of The Adidam Revelation* (consisting of five Courses, which, together, present a comprehensive overview of Avatar Adi Da's entire Wisdom-Teaching) and *The Companions Of The True Dawn Horse* (consisting of seventeen Courses, each of which elaborates on particular topics from *The Dawn Horse Testament*).

> *The "Source-Texts"*
> *(or True-Water-Bearers)*
> *Of My Avataric Divine Wisdom-Teaching*
> *(In Its Twenty-Three Courses Of*
> *True-Water-Born Speech)—*
> *With [My] Divine Testament*
> *As The Epitome*
> *(or First and Principal Text,*
> *and "Bright" True-Water-Mill)*
> *Among Them—*
> *Are, Together, [My] Sufficient Word—*
> *Given, In Summary,*
> *To You*
> *(and, Therefore, To all).*
>
> —Avatar Adi Da Samraj
> *The Dawn Horse Testament*
> *Of The Ruchira Avatar*

The "Source-Texts" of the Avataric Divine Wisdom-Teaching of Adi Da Samraj (in Its Twenty-Three Courses)

The Dawn Horse Testament Of The Ruchira Avatar
(in Its Single Course)

THE DAWN HORSE TESTAMENT OF THE RUCHIRA AVATAR
The Testament Of Divine Secrets Of The Divine World-Teacher, Ruchira Avatar Adi Da Samraj

The Heart Of The Adidam Revelation
(in Its Five Courses)

1. AHAM DA ASMI
   (BELOVED, I AM DA)
   The "Late-Time" Avataric Revelation Of The True and Spiritual Divine Person (The egoless Personal Presence Of Reality and Truth, Which Is The Only Real Acausal God)

2. RUCHIRA AVATARA GITA
   (THE AVATARIC WAY OF THE DIVINE HEART-MASTER)
   The "Late-Time" Avataric Revelation Of The Great Secret Of The Divinely Self-Revealed Way That Most Perfectly Realizes The True and Spiritual Divine Person (The egoless Personal Presence Of Reality and Truth, Which Is The Only Real Acausal God)

3. DA LOVE-ANANDA GITA
   (THE FREE AVATARIC GIFT OF THE DIVINE LOVE-BLISS)
   The "Late-Time" Avataric Revelation Of The Great Means To Worship and To Realize The True and Spiritual Divine Person (The egoless Personal Presence Of Reality and Truth, Which Is The Only Real Acausal God)

4. HRIDAYA ROSARY
   (FOUR THORNS OF HEART-INSTRUCTION)
   The "Late-Time" Avataric Revelation Of The Universally Tangible Divine Spiritual Body, Which Is The Supreme Agent Of The Great Means To Worship and To Realize The True and Spiritual Divine Person (The egoless Personal Presence Of Reality and Truth, Which Is The Only Real Acausal God)

5. ELEUTHERIOS
   (THE ONLY TRUTH THAT SETS THE HEART FREE)
   The "Late-Time" Avataric Revelation Of The "Perfect Practice" Of The Great Means To Worship and To Realize The True and Spiritual Divine Person (The egoless Personal Presence Of Reality and Truth, Which Is The Only Real Acausal God)

The Companions Of The True Dawn Horse
(in Their Seventeen Courses)

1. REAL (ACAUSAL) GOD IS THE INDIVISIBLE ONENESS OF UNBROKEN LIGHT
   Reality, Truth, and The "Non-Creator" God In The Universal Transcendental Spiritual Way Of Adidam

   THE TRANSMISSION OF DOUBT
   Transcending Scientific Materialism

2. THE TRULY HUMAN NEW WORLD-CULTURE OF UNBROKEN REAL-GOD-MAN
   The Eastern Versus The Western Traditional Cultures Of Humankind, and The Unique New Non-Dual Culture Of The Universal Transcendental Spiritual Way Of Adidam

   SCIENTIFIC PROOF OF THE EXISTENCE OF GOD WILL SOON BE ANNOUNCED BY THE WHITE HOUSE!
   Prophetic Wisdom about the Myths and Idols of Mass Culture and Popular Religious Cultism, the New Priesthood of Scientific and Political Materialism, and the Secrets of Enlightenment Hidden in the Human Body

   NOT-TWO IS PEACE
   The Ordinary People's Way of Global Cooperative Order

3. THE ONLY COMPLETE WAY TO REALIZE THE UNBROKEN LIGHT OF REAL (ACAUSAL) GOD
   An Introductory Overview Of The "Radical" Divine Way Of The Universal Transcendental Spiritual Way Of Adidam

4. THE KNEE OF LISTENING
   The Divine Ordeal Of The Avataric Incarnation Of Conscious Light— The Spiritual Autobiography Of The Avataric Great Sage, Adi Da Samraj

5. THE DIVINE SIDDHA-METHOD OF THE RUCHIRA AVATAR
   The Divine Way Of Adidam Is An ego-Transcending Relationship, Not An ego-Centric Technique

   Volume I: MY "BRIGHT" WORD

   Volume II: MY "BRIGHT" SIGHT

   Volume III: MY "BRIGHT" FORM

   Volume IV: MY "BRIGHT" ROOM

6. THE "FIRST ROOM" TRILOGY

BOOK ONE:
THE MUMMERY BOOK
*A Parable Of Divine Tragedy, Told By Means Of
A Self-Illuminated Illustration Of The Totality Of Mind*

BOOK TWO:
THE SCAPEGOAT BOOK
*The Previously Secret Dialogue on the Avatarically Given Divine Way of
"Perfect-Knowledge"-Only, Once-Spoken in a Single Night of Conversation,
Between the Captive Divine Avatar and Great Sage, Raymond Darling, and
His Captor, the Great Fool, and False Teacher, and Notoriously Eccentric
Super-Criminal, Evelyn Disk—Herein Fully Given, Without Evelyn Disk's
Later and Famous and self-Serving Revisions, but Exactly As They Were
Originally Tape-Recorded, by Evelyn Disk himself, in the First Room, at the
State Mental Facility, near God's End, and Presented in Exact Accordance
with the Recent Revelatory and Complete Recounting, Given to the Waiting
World of Intelligent and Receptive Persons, by Meridian Smith, Who Was,
As Usual, Inexplicably Present*

BOOK THREE:
THE HAPPENINE BOOK
*The Childhood Teachings and The End-of-Childhood Revelations of The Famous
"Infant Sage", Raymond Darling—Compiled from Raymond Darling's
Original Handwritten Manuscripts, and Privately Held Tape-Recordings,
Discovered in The First Room By His True Servant-Devotee, Meridian Smith,
After The Miraculous Disappearance of The Avataric Great Sage*

7. HE-AND-SHE IS ME
*The Indivisibility Of Consciousness and Light In The Divine Body Of
The Ruchira Avatar*

8. RUCHIRA SHAKTIPAT YOGA
*The Divine (and Not Merely Cosmic) Spiritual Baptism In The Divine Way
Of Adidam*

9. RUCHIRA TANTRA YOGA
*The Physical-Spiritual (and Truly Religious) Method Of Mental, Emotional,
Sexual, and Whole Bodily Health and Enlightenment In The Divine Way
Of Adidam*

EASY DEATH
Spiritual Wisdom on the Ultimate Transcending of Death and Everything Else

CONSCIOUS EXERCISE AND THE TRANSCENDENTAL SUN
*The Universal ego-Transcending Principle of Love Applied to Exercise and
the Method of Common Physical Action—A Science of Whole Bodily Wisdom,
or True Emotion, Intended Most Especially for Those Engaged in Religious
(and, in Due Course, Spiritual) Life*

THE EATING GORILLA COMES IN PEACE
The Universal ego-Transcending Principle of Love Applied to Diet and the Regenerative Discipline of True Health

LOVE OF THE TWO-ARMED FORM
The Practice of Right Regenerative Sexuality in Ordinary Life, and the Transcending of Sexuality in True Spiritual Practice

10. THE SEVEN STAGES OF LIFE
    Transcending The Six Stages Of egoic Life, and Realizing The ego-Transcending Seventh Stage Of Life, In The Divine Way Of Adidam

11. THE ALL-COMPLETING AND FINAL DIVINE REVELATION TO HUMANKIND
    A Summary Description Of The Supreme Yoga Of The Seventh Stage Of Life In The Divine Way Of Adidam

12. WHAT, WHERE, WHEN, HOW, WHY, AND WHO TO REMEMBER TO BE HAPPY
    A Simple Explanation Of The Divine Way Of Adidam (For Children, and Everyone Else)

13. NO SEEKING / MERE BEHOLDING
    The Always Primary Practice Of The Divine Way Of Adidam

14. SANTOSHA ADIDAM
    The Essential Summary Of The Divine Way Of Adidam

15. THE LION SUTRA
    The "Perfect Practice" Teachings In The Divine Way Of Adidam

16. THE OVERNIGHT REVELATION OF CONSCIOUS LIGHT
    The "My House" Discourses On The Indivisible Tantra Of Adidam

17. THE BASKET OF TOLERANCE
    The Perfect Guide To Perfectly Unified Understanding Of The One and Great Tradition Of Humankind, and Of The Divine Way Of Adidam As The Perfect Completing Of The One and Great Tradition Of Humankind

    UP?
    Beyond the Beginner's Spiritual Way of Saint Jesus and the Traditions of Mystical Cosmic Ascent via Spirit-Breath

    IS
    The "Perfect Knowledge" of Reality and The "Radical" Way to Realize It

    NIRVANASARA
    The Essence of the Teaching of Reality in the Realistic Traditions of Buddhism, in the Idealistic Traditions of Advaita Vedanta, and in the "Radical" World-Teaching of Adidam

We invite you to find out more about Avatar Adi Da Samraj and the Way of Adidam

■ Find out about our courses, seminars, events, and retreats by calling the regional center nearest you.

AMERICAS	**EUROPE-AFRICA**	**AUSTRALIA**
12040 N. Seigler Rd.	Annendaalderweg 10	P.O. Box 244
Middletown, CA	6105 AT Maria Hoop	Kew 3101
95461 USA	The Netherlands	Victoria
1-707-928-4936	**31 (0)20 468 1442**	**1800 ADIDAM**
		(1800-234-326)
THE UNITED	**PACIFIC-ASIA**	
KINGDOM	12 Seibel Road	**INDIA**
uk@adidam.org	Henderson	Shree Love-Ananda Marg
0845-330-1008	Auckland 1008	Rampath, Shyam Nagar Extn.
	New Zealand	Jaipur–302 019, India
	64-9-838-9114	**91 (141) 2293080**

E-MAIL: **correspondence@adidam.org**

■ Order books, tapes, CDs, DVDs, and videos by and about Avatar Adi Da Samraj.

1-877-770-0772 (from within North America)
1-707-928-6653 (from outside North America)
order online: **www.dawnhorsepress.com**

■ Visit us online:
www.adidam.org
Explore the online community of Adidam and discover more about Avatar Adi Da and the Way of Adidam.